The Last True Story

of *Titanic*

by *James G. Clary*

D1496585

Domhan Books

This book is dedicated to the late Jack Grimm, pioneer underwater Explorer, who first found the Titanic.

Copyright text and pictures by James G. Clary 1998

ISBN: 1-58345-000-9

Published by Domhan Books

The word Domhan, pronounced DOW-ann is the Irish word for universe. Our vision is to bring you books in all genres from new writers all over the world.

In the UK:
3 Killyvilly Grove
Enniskillen
N. Ireland
BT 74 4RT

In the USA:
9511 Shore Road, Suite 514
Brooklyn, NY 11209

The Last True Story of *Titanic*
By James Clary

Table of Contents

-The Fire and Explosion
-Did the Great Ship Break in Two?
-Inferior Metal and Rivets
-Saved by the Iceberg?
-Make-shift Rafts
-A Bow-on Strike
-Binoculars and a Searchlight
-Reversing to Suck Out Water

Illustrations start after page 73.

Acknowledgments

I wish to express my heartfelt gratitude to my Creator and the following institutions and individuals for their kind efforts to make this book and the artwork within both possible and historically accurate:

The Good Lord who blessed me with the talents that I have; the late Jack Grimm, pioneer *Titanic* explorer; the late Edwina (Troutt) McKenzie, *Titanic* survivor; Winnifred Van Tongerloo, *Titanic* Survivor; the late George Thomas,*Titanic* survivor; Thomas McKluskie, Harland and Wolff historian; Thomas Needham, Francis Searchlights, Bolton, United Kingdom; Mariners' Museum, Newport News, VA; Ulster *Titanic* Society, Bangor Co. Down, Northern Ireland; University of Michigan Astronomy Department; Nelson Zimmer, Naval Architect; and Siobhan McNally, Lakeside Literary Agency.

Prologue

Although at first many denied it, a giant ocean liner was dying. The superstitious nodded their heads, knowing her fate had already been sealed. After striking the giant iceberg, initial concerns were quickly calmed when the vessel resumed her course. But the freezing Atlantic waters were creeping up to the forecastle head as the massive vessel, with all her lights aglow, slowly, almost imperceptibly, sank at the bow.

Amid the deafening and ominous roar of escaping steam, baffled passengers, who were at first told there was nothing to worry about, were now advised to don life jackets and proceed to the lifeboats. Women and children peered at loved ones left aboard as they were haphazardly lowered into the ice-chilled darkness far below. The sea was dead calm, the sky was unusually clear, and the orchestra continued to play as if to say all was well.

As the grand, unsinkable luxury liner slowly foundered to her watery grave, she generated reverberations that would shock the world at the time and mesmerize man forever.

Chapter One

The Giants Are Born

Three giants they built 'n spared no cost,
And then the famous one was lost.
With too few lifeboats she went to sea.
The unsinkable sank. How could this be?

It is one of the most awe-inspiring words in the world's vocabulary. *Titanic.* It is difficult to find any corner of the globe not familiar with the great *Titanic.* Her fascination captures the imagination of all. Countless scholars and enthusiasts spanning a wide age-group search for and collect anything and everything connected with the ship. Children not only seriously collect *Titanic* memorabilia but also can intelligently converse on the subject as well. And even after she has finally been seen again in the depths of her dark tomb, with many of her secrets revealed, her mystique lives on.

This legendary aura began with what many called the engineering feat of the twentieth century: the building of the grandest ocean liners ever known. Three ships would be built for the White Star Line, at the Belfast, Ireland, yard of Harland and Wolff. They would be like no others before them, both in size and splendor.

When Bruce Ismay, managing director of the White Star Line, met with Harland and Wolff officials in 1907, it was to plan for the construction of three 45,000 ton vessels, the largest ever designed, each capable of speeds of at least twenty-two knots. The Cunard liners, *Lusitania* and *Mauretania,* had just come into service that year, and Cunard maintained a tight grip on the lion's share of the North Atlantic trade. At 31,000 tons each, these majestic vessels were not only larger, but also much faster than any vessel in the White Star fleet. Their reign was undisputed, for these two queens held fast the coveted North Atlantic speed prize: the Blue Ribband. Each could dash through the seas at an astounding speed of twenty-two to twenty-six knots, and would frequently entertain friendly rivalry by shaving time off each other's crossings, thereby passing the speed record back and forth between them. The *Mauretania* would boast of being the fastest Atlantic liner until 1929.

The White Star Line, in order to stay competitive and capture a larger piece of the Atlantic travel market, contracted for three new vessels that would surpass the magnificence of anything afloat. They would be named *Olympic, Titanic,* and *Gigantic.* The *Olympic* and *Titanic* were to be operational by 1910, with the *Gigantic* to follow.

Also unprecedented in enormity was the creation of what became known as the Great Gantry at the Harland and Wolff yard. Two giant slips, formed by combining three smaller slips, would soon become the beehive of activity where construction of the three behemoths would take place. The huge gantry was erected over these slips supported by three rows of support towers spaced 121 feet apart. Each of these three rows of towers contained eleven towers spaced along their length eighty feet apart. Across the very top of the rows of towers were massive girders that stretched across the berths and served as pathways for cranes. Electric lifts allowed access to the upper areas of the structure. The enormous framework of girders, crossbeams, and supports, appeared as the skeleton of a great skyscraper and was in itself a wonder to behold.

Crouching against the cold and crammed together on one of the many two-deck trolley buses, workers being shuttled to the yard once again caught the familiar sight of the giant hull No. 401 through the early morning mist. The *Titanic,* in its early stages of construction, would be their destination and work place for the long day ahead. Flowing through the streets and sidewalks around the complex, the vast army of laborers approached the yard, like an endless trail of ants approaching their hill.

For the weary laborers, the excitement of working on the largest vessels ever built had perhaps worn off because of the routine of the job. But the well-known project still attracted the eyes and ears of the citizens surrounding the site, and also those around the world, who were utterly captivated by the magnitude of the task.

Of the thirty- to forty-thousand laborers and tradesmen employed by Harland and Wolff, as many as three to four thousand were involved in the construction of the *Titanic* at any given time. Because a great percentage of these workers lived in the countryside many miles away, the company provided modest one- to three-bedroom homes near the yard for three or four shillings a week.

With the nine-hour work day beginning at 7:50 a.m., shipyard workers had to rise early enough for a hearty breakfast to fortify themselves for the many exhausting hours ahead.

Passing the time-keeper's windows one by one, the swarm of laborers placed their wooden block stamped with their employee number in the proper slot to signify they were present for duty.

Arriving at the work area, the refreshing but fleeting whiff of the sea would be taken over by a mixture of the pungent odors of super-heated steel, lubricating oil, and coal-fire smoke that soon filled the air.

There were no food concessions or lunch wagons at the site, so each man brought his own sustenance, to be hastily devoured either during a ten minute break at 10:00 a.m. or during the thirty short minutes allowed for lunch.

The winter temperatures could be sub- or near-zero.

The work was monotonous, back-breaking, and freezing. But there was still great pride in the work force knowing that they were building the largest ships in the world. It was also a golden opportunity for some: you could earn £2.00 a week ($10.00 US) and increase that to £5.00 ($25.00 US) by working all night Friday and all day Saturday.

During inclement weather the tradesmen who worked in the warmer surroundings of the platers' sheds were the envy of those who worked outside. Here the enormous steel plates, or sheets as they were called, were fashioned, punched, drilled, marked, and stored for eventual installation onto the ribs of the giant vessel taking shape nearby.

Even better were the working conditions in the warm and quiet environment of the mammoth mould loft, where a football-field-sized ballroom-type floor was carefully marked and laid out to configure the various pieces of the great ship in tenth scale.

Work in the joiner's shop too was more bearable. Here, hundreds of woodworkers plied their handiwork using the finest hardwoods to fabricate the elegant panels, carvings, and trimmings to be fitted into the ship's interior.

In the winter, working conditions outside were harsh. With little protection from the elements, the routine was cold, and one enveloped in the constant, deafening din common to the yard. The noise produced by the giant cranes constantly maneuvering their loads, their motors whining at high pitch, or laboring traction engines moving steel, was dreadful. But drowning out even this clamor was the phenomenal and incessant banging of hundreds upon hundreds of hammers swung by the riveters at their work, many of them competing to set the most rivets during their shift. The *Titanic* and *Olympic* would embody three million, one-and-a-quarter inch rivets each, weighing around twelve hundred tons per ship—a half-million in their double bottoms alone—sixty percent of which were hand-riveted.

According to Harland and Wolff Historian, Tom McLuskie, twelve men, six per side, could completely rivet in place a thirty-by six-foot plate in two to three minutes. Each of these plates, depending on whether it was single, double, triple, or quadruple riveted, might contain as many as one-hundred and forty rivets. If some of the holes in the giant one-inch thick plates did not exactly line up to accept the rivets, the holes were reamed to fit using gigantic pneumatic drills.

Pride in the work was obvious, but there was also heavy rivalry among the workers too. Many of the men endeavored to outdo others in their specific tasks in order to counter the monotony of their work. John Moir, the world champion riveter, still holds the record for manually setting 11,209 rivets in a single nine-hour period at the rate of twenty-three and a-half every minute! Moir worked at the neighboring shipyard of Workman Clark Ltd. in Belfast, and outperformed his nearest rival, riveter John Lowry at Harland and Wolff (who is believed to have worked on the *Titanic*), by more than four thousand rivets. Even John Lowry's second place feat seems unbelievable. To accomplish this Lowry would have had to set about thirteen rivets a minute for nine hours, non-stop.

No wonder that industrial deafness was rampant in those days amongst the workers in that type of environment. Other injuries also plagued the work force besides deafness. If your job was that of a "heater boy" you could have at least kept relatively warm. These lads manned the coal-fired, portable rivet furnaces, a rolling blacksmith's forge if you will, that heated fifty to sixty rivets at a time to the white hot stage. The searing rivets were picked up with tongs by the heater boy and tossed, sometimes high in the air, to the "catch boys," who caught the rivets in a small catch bucket and placed them in the chosen hole to be hammered fast in position. But quite often the white hot rivets were accidentally dropped to land on those below, causing severe burns.

During extreme low temperatures, when compressed air was blown into tight areas for ventilation, those inside the plating who butted up the opposite end of the rivet—"the holder-on"—as he was called, could easily be susceptible to frostbite or "white finger disease," caused by the blast of frigid air in contact with bare skin.

If all this clatter and hammering in the yard wasn't enough, should this noise happen to briefly cease for a break or work delay, the aggravating sound of twenty to thirty-thousand chirping starlings constantly perched in the high reaches of the giant gantry presented yet another almost unbearable racket. And to further hinder the work, it was common after a few days' holiday to return to the job to find an inch of bird droppings blanketing everything beneath the roosts.

By March 31, 1909, from a vantage point high atop the dizzying height of the gantry, one could better grasp the enormity of the *Titanic*. The completed three-foot-six-inch high keel that stretched nearly the full length of ship, gave you some idea of the behemoth that was coming.

Without ceremony or fanfare, workmen had placed a single bronze penny at the exact center of the keel between the keel and the keel plate. Sealed there forever, this age- old tradition meant to guarantee good luck undoubtedly offered assurance that the vessel would be favored. There was talk among the men gathered for tea around the rivet furnaces that this vessel would be unsinkable, and perhaps they thought that she would need all the good luck she could muster.

The *Olympic* in the adjacent slip was already fully framed and thereby upstaging the *Titanic* because by then one could begin to fully see the tremendous size of *Titanic*'s twin.

The endless array of stockpiles of marked plating, gigantic castings, brackets, and frames, although a routine sight to the workmen, would simply baffle those unaccustomed to the tremendous size of the stock and the complex inventory of material on hand in the yard. There rested the seventy-ton stern frame, soon to be towering upright to offer the first hint of the shape of the *Titanic*'s hull. Nearby, a ninety-two foot, one-and-a-quarter ton beam, the longest girder in the ship, dwarfed those working around it.

The mammoth rudder alone, comprised of six separate sections, weighed as much as a hundred of today's automobiles. This seventy-foot long, fifteen-foot wide mass of steel, when installed on the ship, would appear tiny in comparison to the immensity of the vessel.

A vast array of other shops both on and off the site all contributed to the manufacture of the fittings, furnishings, and the working systems required for the new ships. Material for plating, plumbing stock, electrical components, pumps, generators, paint, tools, and countless other accoutrements were trucked, shipped, or brought to the yard by rail from nearly all points of the British Isles.

All these thousands of pieces of the giant's puzzle, fashioned at, or brought to the work site at the proper time for installation must have also represented giant headaches for those responsible in assuring the timely progress of the work.

While there was never any promotional or advertising claim by the White Star Line to boast that the *Titanic* was unsinkable, there began to circulate an unshakable belief in this integrity. Not with regard to the *Olympic* mind you, just the *Titanic*. Why this occurred is surely a mystery because both ships were to be, except for a few minor details, exact twins. Was it a popular claim brought about, embellished, and widely spread after the *Titanic* sank, and because it sank?

If one would search for a definitive answer as to how this unsinkable myth began you would find it in an excerpt in the midsummer, 1911, edition of the British shipping trade journal, *The Shipbuilder*. In describing the operation of the watertight doors on both the *Titanic* and the *Olympic*, it stated that, "in the event of accident, or at any time when it may be considered advisable, the captain can, by simply moving an electric switch, instantly close the doors throughout and make the vessel practically unsinkable."

Was there, is there, such a thing as an unsinkable ship? Could a vessel be so well-constructed as to be completely unsinkable? The closest a ship ever came to approaching that integrity was surely not the *Titanic*. It was an earlier giant, *The Great Eastern,* built years ahead of its time by "The Little Giant," Isambard Kingdom Brunel, in 1857. This six-hundred and ninety-three-foot leviathan, built in England on the Thames, had two hulls, one inside the other with a three foot space between them. This double bottom was heavily braced and extended to six feet above the waterline. She was proclaimed as nearly unsinkable as engineering experts could make her. She had a long, dark, and unprofitable career, however, and was scrapped in 1889. But of course she never hit an iceberg. The only bright spot in her life was her participation in the laying of one of the Trans-Atlantic cables.

The new vessels would be comprised of nine decks including the orlop or lowest deck. The hulls were divided into sixteen watertight compartments, and divided by fifteen watertight bulkheads. According to the planned design, the vessels could remain afloat with any two compartments flooded. For further safety, each vessel was fitted with a cellular five-foot-three-inch deep (a foot deeper in the reciprocating engine rooms) double bottom that extended only to the sides of the vessel.

When the *Olympic* was launched on October 20, 1910, only the plating had been completed on the *Titanic*, so it was the *Olympic* that attracted the most admiration and attention. There sat the gleaming white hull of the *Olympic,* with her name proudly displayed on her bow, compared to the black, unfinished, and nameless hull of the *Titanic*.

When the *Olympic* was launched on October 20, 1910, Without complication and within seven months of her launch, the *Olympic* had been fitted out, sent through her trials, and pressed into service. However, shortly after she was in operation, she had to return to Belfast for repairs which delayed the completion of the *Titanic*. Again, the *Titanic* bowed graciously to allow her sister to go first.

One would expect jubilation or hurrahs when the last rivet was finally set in the last rivet hole on the *Titanic*. It would seem to be the perfect occasion for a company-wide party or at least some kind of celebration. However, it was most likely achieved quietly and without notice because the workmen considered it dreadfully unlucky to ever say that the ship or any part thereof was finished.

Chapter Two

The Unlucky Launch

Standing there on the greasy ways,
Was the largest vessel of the days.
Thousands watched and amid the din,
Without a word they shoved her in.

To see the *Titanic* at this stage of her construction, even though she was ready for launch, many would have perceived her as only half-completed. Her hull was fully-formed, she was slick with her first coat of black paint, and her anchors were even snugged up on her bows.

However, much of her superstructure, including her masts, funnels, internal systems, furnishings, decoration, electrical wiring, and equipment, had yet to be installed. All of this work would soon be accomplished at her fitting-out. This cavernous hull, practically an empty shell, was really all that was ready for the proposed launch.

During my many years of study on maritime superstition, I found among shipbuilders, shipowners, and sailors, varying pockets of belief and disbelief. These views exist right up to the present time. Some will simply look the other way with regard to the foolishness of superstition, ancient traditions, practice, or custom. Others gravely regard, follow, and adhere to these beliefs with an almost religious fervor.

In maritime communities of old, shipbuilders carefully followed launching practices and custom to ensure that every detail of the event went smoothly, without any incident to blemish the ritual, and in turn blemish the new ship.

Sometimes great pains were taken to bring harmony

and favor to the launch. Many shipbuilders believed that the launch of the vessel was far more important than the actual building of the vessel itself. Some shipbuilders even went so far as to cast bits of fish upon the water adjacent to the launch site. Sea gulls would then be cheerfully on the wing, and dolphins would be lured into playing about. All this was done in the hope of attaining perfect harmony for a favored launch.

If any accident, injury, or death was associated with the launch, if wine or champagne was not spilled, if the vessel was not given a name, or lacked the proper ceremony, it was believed that the vessel would be marked with an indelible stain of bad luck. Heaven forbid should anyone ever contemplate launching a ship on a Friday.

Launching ceremonies in some circles are still a very serious and important event. At the General Dynamics Electric Boat Division at Groton, Connecticut, for example, over a hundred submarines were built and launched, all with careful plans to ensure a lucky launch and a safe and well-favored boat. (In submariner's jargon a sub is referred to as a boat).

The lady-sponsor will visit the shipyard days in advance of the event to practice for the ritual with weighted bottles. There will be extra bottles of champagne on the reviewing stand should the sponsor accidentally drop the one intended for the launching. If the boat should happen to move away from the reviewing stand before it is smacked or christened, a second lady-sponsor aboard the new boat is expected to stand ready to smash her bottle over the bow before the ship touches the water.

On a smaller scale, as recently as 1992, boat builders on the island of Carriacou in the West Indies were still performing the ancient rite of sprinkling the decks of fishing boats with the blood of he-goats for good luck.

Harland and Wolff historian, Tom McLuskie, relates that his company, in business since 1861, always had launch-

ing and christening ceremonies for their new ships, and that
they continue that tradition to this day. Usually a lady- sponsor will christen a new vessel with the act of breaking the
champagne bottle over the bow along with a blessing to give
the ship her name.

I queried him about this specifically because some
Titanic accounts tell us that Harland and Wolff did not believe in such ceremonies. His response was that the White
Star Line did not want christening ceremonies or the like for
any of their ships. They never did. The decision in these
matters was left up to the owner, but Harland and Wolff has
been christening their own new vessels since the company
began.

To the White Star line, the idea of a ceremonial launch
and a blessing for their new vessels was simply not a consid-
eration.

This blatant disregard of the old customs may have
been shrugged off by the White Star Line, but to the workers
who built these vessels and to the men who sailed them, there
would have been anything but indifference. Since the *Titanic* had been built by predominantly Irish laborers, who
were considered to be one of the most superstitious nation-
alities of all, it is a wonder the workmen who built her and
the sailors who manned her would even associate themselves
with a vessel considered to be so unlucky.

But on Wednesday, May 31, 1911, with fair skies at
least, all the shipping company dignitaries, workmen and their
families, and hundreds of other distinguished visitors flocked
to the yard to see the great ship launched. Among the prin-
ciples on hand were J. Pierpont Morgan, head of International
Mercantile Marine, the company that controlled the White
Star Line; William James Pirrie, chairman of Harland and
Wolff; Thomas Andrews, the *Titanic*'s designer; Alexander
Carlisle, who was responsible for the interior decorating and
the life-saving equipment; and J. Bruce Ismay, head of the

White Star Line.

Despite the great technical planning required to accomplish the launch, and the fact that over 100,000 spectators watched the event, including the special honored guests who had made long journeys to be there, the launch of the *Titanic* was for the most part a *non-event*.

Mandated by the White Star Line, the low-key procedure for the launch began at 12:13 p.m. When all was ready, Lord Pirrie simply gave the calm order to the launch foreman. Yes, there was a tumultuous roar from the crowd when the ship first moved, along with the expected and clamorous total chorus of, "There she goes". But that was it.

There were no grand words spoken over her by any dignitary, no pageantry to formally give her her name, no bottle of champagne broken across her great bow, no blessing, no ceremony. The great *Titanic* was never properly christened!

Far worse, immediately before the launch, as the giant black hull had sat there motionless for the last time, the legs of workman, James Dobbins, were crushed beneath her. Dobbins had been cutting away some of the last wooden supports, which crumbled and pinned him helplessly underneath the great hull. His workmates were able to pull him free at the last moment before the ship slid into the water, but the man died the next day. It was the worst possible thing to have happen at a launch. A death directly associated with the event was surely one of the worst possible omens.

It was therefore believed by the superstitious, that due to this death, the lack of ceremony and a formal christening, with no giving of the name, that the great liner *Titanic* was doomed from the very start.

But oblivious to the superstitious rumblings, the *Titanic* now floated peacefully in her element, reaching a speed down the ways of twelve knots. The entire process had taken no more than sixty-two seconds. Special heavy anchors which had been sunk in the river bottom and attached to seven-inch steel cables restrained and gently stopped the vessel at a distance of no more than her own length.

One final event occurred shortly after the brief launch which, in retrospect, has been perceived by many as a sign that the great *Titanic* had been doomed from the start. Even on what should have been her greatest day, during her finest hour, the *Titanic* was snubbed. The interest of the multitudes who came there to see her spectacular launch was quickly diverted by the officials at the ceremony to an inspection of the *Titanic*'s sister ship, the sparkling new *Olympic*.

Chapter Three

Fitting Out

Tradesmen swarmed over the giant hulk,
With trainloads of gear, trim, and bulk.
Filling the leviathan where she lay,
At a feverish pitch for her sailing day.

Moved to the nearby fitting out basin, the great work force that had carefully molded her great hull, now concentrated on transforming her bare form into a complete ship. Fitted into her interior came an intricate honey-comb of bulkheads, partitions, corridors, and companionways through which was threaded endless miles of electrical wiring. Tons of gear and components to run her vast systems of propulsion, steering, lighting, refrigeration, heat, and ventilation all came aboard to be fitted into place.

The shipyard's giant floating crane capable of raising one hundred and fifty tons lifted aboard her mammoth engines and boilers. She would carry twenty-nine, fifteen foot nine-inch diameter boilers. Twenty-four of these would be double-ended with a length of twenty foot. The five single-ended boilers measured eleven-foot nine inches long. The twenty-nine boilers would contain a total of 159 furnaces which soon would be fed tons of coal to produce the steam for her engines.

Work progressed as well on her superstructure, deck houses and wooden deck. Over two thousand windows, sidelights, and decorative panes of glass, seemingly enough for a skyscraper, were also installed. Lavish tiles, rivers of carpeting, fine wood panels, elegant trim, and elaborate refinements, carefully built into her interiors, breathed more life into the ship.

At almost a feverish pace the work continued through the summer and fall of 1911, but was interrupted because of a collision between the *Olympic* and the HMS *Hawke*. This caused delay as workers were diverted to the accident repairs and other modifications on the *Olympic*.

By the end of November construction on the *Titanic* resumed, and by the end of January 1912, she was nearly finished. With her masts and funnels in place, she at last presented the grand appearance of a completed liner.

Although Atlantic travel was heavy in those years, passengers sailing the high seas before the *Titanic* disaster could not have been entirely without ocean travel fears. In the fifty years preceding the loss of the *Titanic*, no less than twelve vessels were sunk with the loss of over five hundred lives, all due to collision with icebergs.

On January 22, 1909, the White Star liner *Republic,* collided in fog with the Lloyd Italiano liner *Florida* off Nantucket. Tons of sea water poured into the pierced hull of the *Republic,* causing her to sink after remaining afloat for nearly thirty-nine hours. The Marconi wireless, which had just recently come into use, was credited for the success of the greatest sea rescue of the time. Miraculously, out of the sixteen hundred and fifty passengers and crew from both vessels, only five lives were lost.

Other ocean fears such as lack of vessel stability, severe weather, and threat of fire were certainly justified concerns as well.

It was a principle endeavor then for shipowners to instill safety and security in the minds of their customers. To help calm these fears, ship design employed the four-stack look of the times. A symbol of strength and security, the four funnels offered the look of stability along with the appearance of utmost majesty.

This four-funnel design characteristic also carried over

into the Great Lakes when in 1912, the Cleveland & Buffalo Transit Company employed the four stack look of four funnels on the *Seeandbee*, a five-hundred-foot long 98.6-foot beam vessel, the largest side-wheel steamer in the world at the time.

And so the *Titanic*, like the Cunard liners *Lusitania* and *Mauretania*, would also carry four stacks. Wide enough at their widest dimension to accept three automobiles side by side, the elliptical cross section of these huge funnels measured twenty-four feet six inches by nineteen feet, and they stood eighty one feet above the boat deck.

To announce her presence, on each of the four stacks, were fitted the largest triple-bell whistles ever made. Having a nine-inch, a twelve-inch, and a center fifteen-inch diameter bell, each whistle measured fifty-and-one-half inches high by forty-two inches wide and weighed six hundred and seventy-five pounds apiece. One can only imagine the harmonious and distinctive bellow that must have emanated from these unique whistles.

As standard shipboard gear, she carried three glistening brass bells, the largest of which was twenty-three inches in diameter located on the foremast. Those who heard the melodious chime as it struck the ship's time, during her short life, must have witnessed a comforting "all is well" feeling.

Her great masts too were truly something to marvel at. Reaching skyward these great spires were raked aft at just the right angle to offer the illusion that the vessel was swiftly underway. To the one-hundred and one-foot, six-inch foremast was fitted the generous crow's nest accessible by way of a fifty-foot interior ladder. The main mast towered ninety-seven feet, five inches.

Hung in a graceful curve nearly two hundred and twenty-five feet above the keel swung the wireless aerials spanning the great distance between the masts.

With a Marconi wireless system more powerful than

on any other merchant vessel at the time, it provided a communication range of two hundred and fifty to four hundred miles during most atmospheric conditions. It also had an extreme range of receiving and transmitting of up to two thousand miles at night.

The race toward her debut continued as legions of craftsmen poured over her in almost frantic determination. Finish carpenters, electricians, carpet installers, painters, detailers, plumbers, tile layers, and decorators labored around each other, all vying for available space or opportunity in which to complete their work.

Already hung in place beneath Welin double-acting davits were sixteen wooden, thirty-foot long lifeboats. These davits could deploy three boats each, and were known for their ease of operation and space saving characteristics.

Although designer Alexander Carlisle presented plans for both a sixty-four and a thirty-two lifeboat arrangement, the owners and builders instead decided on only sixteen boats. The decision was surely one with cost saving in mind, but it was also supported by an 1894, British Board of Trade regulation that based lifeboat capacity on the tonnage of vessels of the time. With the size of 1912 era vessels far exceeding the size of those stipulated in the antiquated regulation, the law was stretched somewhat to say the least. Nonetheless the outdated guidelines required *Titanic* to provide a 9,625 cubic foot lifeboat capacity. Her sixteen boats provided a 9,752 cubic foot capacity, and along with the installation of four canvas Englehardt collapsible boats her total of twenty lifeboats would provide a capacity of 11,327.9 cubic feet or enough to exceed and comply with the Board of Trade regulation.

This meant that according to their designed maximum capacity, the twenty lifeboats could carry a total of only 1,178 people. Even so, the Board of Trade officials would soon certify the *Titanic*'s capability to carry a total of 3,547 passengers and crewmen.

How could this very obvious disparity in the numbers be overlooked? Were the powers to be that confident in believing that their vessel was truly unsinkable? They surely must have been. It was indeed a classic example of how the technology of the time raced far ahead of the laws that governed the populace.

By the end of March, although the last finishing touches were being attended to by carpenters, decorators, and painters, the long construction phase of *Titanic*'s life was nearly over. Her lighting fixtures, wall sconces, and grand candelabra were in place, passenger elevators were finished and tested, kitchen equipment was in order, bed linens and mattresses were aboard, and all her floors were polished.

As the anticipated April 10th sailing date drew near, a last minute design change was brought about because of *Olympic* passenger complaints. The annoyance of sea spray on that vessel was bothering passengers who strolled along the promenade on A deck. So considerate were the owners to soothe even the slightest passenger distaste that the matter was quickly addressed and the change adopted. Almost unheard of at this late stage of construction, the forward A deck open windows were removed and replaced with sliding glass windows that would allow first class travellers to promenade in comfort. This eleventh hour design change became the only noticeable feature to distinguish the *Titanic* from the *Olympic*.

At last, with coal aboard and all of her systems checked and in order she stood ready for her trials and the long awaited delivery to her owners.

Chapter Four

Short Trials and On To Southampton

Too rushed to place her on the run,
Unsinkable anyway, the job was done.
Trials too short to know their ship,
Especially for an ill-fated trip.

No matter how seasoned a veteran mariner could be, it is most important for the officers and crew members of a new vessel to become acquainted and familiar with their ship during trials. While they may have been proficiently experienced on many other different vessels, it is necessary for the crew during trials to familiarize themselves with the systems, equipment, handling, and all the intricacies of the vessel undergoing the trials.

That the *Titanic* was indeed in a race with time to meet a scheduled sailing date was certain fact. There was always a rush. No navigation company could make any vessel pay by wasting time. On the other hand, by shortchanging the necessary time for a crew to adequately learn and know their entire ship proficiently, that vessel and the lives of those who sailed on that vessel could be placed in jeopardy. This would be especially true if the "hands on" training involving new or different lifesaving equipment and procedures were neglected or abbreviated.

In light of the tragic comedy of errors surrounding the *Titanic* disaster, which point directly to the lack of crew experience, and in comparison with the time allowed for trials of other large liners, the *Titanic* and her crew were unquestionably short-changed.

Olympic's trials lasted two days, and reportedly went so well, that the shipbuilder and the owners may have been complacent in believing that it was not necessary to put the *Titanic* through the same gamut, being she was such a near twin. Sea trials on the Cunard liners *Mauretania*, *Lusitania*, and *Queen Mary* had each lasted a week or more. *Titanic*'s sea trials would last no more than twelve hours.

Titanic's trials were performed in the Belfast Lough and in the more open waters of the Irish Sea. Aboard were seventy-eight engine room crewmen; forty-one officers and veteran crewmen; two representatives of the White Star Line; Thomas Andrews and Edward Wilding representing Harland and Wolff; the Board of Trade ship surveyor, Francis Carruthers; Jack Phillips and Harold Bride, wireless operators; and several experts to adjust the compasses.

Just after 6:00 a.m. on April 2nd, five big tugs steadied the pristine ship, carefully guiding her away from her basin through Victoria Channel toward the more open waters of the Lough. Heavy black smoke was pouring from her great funnels as steam was ever-building in preparation for the job in which her engines were about to take part.

Can you imagine the moment? The tugs, one by one were cast off, the "I am undergoing trials," burgee was hoisted, and there for just a short while, the great *Titanic* stood by herself quietly in the open waters, magnificent, and seemingly chomping at the bit. The sheer thrill and joy of those who created, formed, and guided her to this point must surely have been unequalled.

The jangle of the engine room telegraph bells acknowledged the bridge command for all ahead slow, and her giant propellers churned for the first time. A faint but steady rhythm reverberated throughout her mass as her engines said, "Yes we have a job to do".

What pride and exultation must have been in the hearts of those aboard to finally see her in action.

She was first run to a speed of almost twenty knots, then allowed to glide slowly to a full stop. Then she was run and stopped several times without the assist of her center turbine engine. Other "rudder only" turning actions such as slowing, increasing speed, and propeller assist functions were then monitored.

While the surveyors documented measurements and observed details, the wireless operators were busy adjusting their system, transmitting and receiving acknowledgments of test messages, and carefully honing that equipment.

During a speed run of twenty-and-one-half knots, on a straight course, the helm was ordered hard over, and the giant made a wide sweeping full circle turn to check her response and angle of heel. The circle in which she turned was measured at 3,850 feet, while travelling forward approximately 2,100 feet.

While some observers sat at lunch in the main dining salon discussing and comparing notes, others monitored the vessel as she moved ahead at dead slow. Next came the crucial stopping test. A marker buoy was set, and the *Titanic* was turned to run past the buoy at full speed. Under careful observation, when the vessel reached a position where the buoy was exactly alongside the bow, signals were relayed to the captain on the bridge to order full astern. With her enormous hull trembling under the stress and her power gradually diminishing from the twenty knot speed she had attained, the observers recorded a forward movement of about 850 yards or just under one-half mile, before she reached a full stop.

In the open waters of the Irish Sea, the *Titanic* ran a straight forty mile course for nearly two hours, turned and ran the same course back averaging about eighteen knots. At one time she attained a speed of twenty-one knots.

As the sun was getting low, the vessel steamed for home, and in the fifteen mile stretch of water in the Lough, the *Titanic* was put into serpentine course manoeuvres as more turns were ordered for one more check of how she handled. In one last test, around 7:00 p.m., after the proud vessel reached Belfast and slowly came to a stop, both port and starboard anchors were dropped. On that evening of April 2, 1912, the approving authority, Francis Carruthers, affixed his signature to the certificate that read, "Good for one year from today". Other documents were signed on behalf of the White Star Line and Harland and Wolff. According to all concerned, the *Titanic* had passed her trials and was thus turned over to her owners.

Shortly after 8:00 p.m., her great anchors were lifted and deckhands scurried as the strict schedule directed all to adhere to their duties quickly. She was soon to depart in time for arrival at Southampton on the midnight tide, almost thirty hours away.

Into the Irish Sea, down St. George's Channel, and west into the English Channel she arrived at Southampton after midnight April 4th, completing the five hundred and seventy- mile passage. She was warped stern first into Berth No. 44 in anticipation of a low water departure at noon on April 10th. But there was a tremendous amount of unfinished work to be accomplished and pressing obstacles to overcome before then.

Not the least of these was the concern for coal. There had been a recently settled but devastating coal strike that closed nearly all the country's mines. The strike, fortunately settled on April 6th, would have restricted all the White Star liners' speed. Shipping had come to a virtual standstill, with every shipping line desperately needing fuel. The trickle-down effects of the stoppage had presented a serious crisis for all. With no time remaining to wait for recently mined coal to reach Southampton, cannibalizing coal was the only alternative left.

Coal left over from the just-departed Olympic, along

with that from five International Mercantile Marine vessels there in Southampton, was sent into *Titanic*'s hungry bunkers. Along with the coal that was left aboard, the *Titanic* would have 6,307 tons of fuel. Over 400 tons of this supply would be consumed in port for the steam required for loading, lighting, and heat.

With the coal problem put to rest, the monumental list of things still to attend to seemed endless. There was the massive task of crew recruitment, made somewhat easier because sailors always preferred work on a new vessel. There was no shortage of willing hands. Many had been without work for some time and the chance to ship on the great *Titanic* was the best incentive of all. Signing on were able seamen, stokers, trimmers, firemen, greasers, stewards, stewardesses, bakers, storekeepers, and a host of others to round out the enormous crew. Most were native of Southampton, with a few from Liverpool and Belfast.

Two of the newly assigned, Stewardess Violet Jessop and Fireman John Priest, deserve a place in the annals of maritime "believe it or not". Jessop and Priest were on the *Olympic* when she collided with the HMS *Hawke* and both would survive the *Titanic* and the sinking of the *Britannic*. Priest would also survive the loss of the *Alcantara* and the *Donegal,* sunk during World War I.

To add to the chaos were the grievances of *Titanic*'s senior officers who, upon coming aboard from Southampton and Belfast, discovered their positions would be restructured to better facilitate operation of the new vessel. This led to disruption and confusion among the officers as to their newly assigned responsibilities. This most likely could have been resolved during the sea trials, had there been sufficient time.

Many staterooms, parlors, and salons were not yet finished. Carpet was still being installed. Painting, window treatments, and the placement of furniture, mattresses, and bedding were still being attended to. *Titanic*'s cranes were constantly hauling aboard everything from tableware, to deck chairs, to the thousands of freight items to be shipped general cargo. A twenty-five horsepower Renault automobile owned by Mr. William Carter, was one of the more unusual items.

Over the Easter weekend, save for now and then wisps of smoke from her funnels, the big ship lay quiet and regal. Even so, schedule would not permit the boarding of Southampton visitors. In order to console the disappointed, the ship was decked out in flags and pennants as a good-will salute to the city.

The work resumed on Monday with just a few days left until the scheduled sailing day, Wednesday, April 10, 1912.

If you can imagine the supplies, staples, provisions, furnishings, beverages, medical and emergency necessities, entertainment accessories, and countless other items necessary to accommodate the citizens of a city with a population of over 3,000, you can begin to see what was required to supply the giant city of a ship.

The enormous quantity of some of the stores brought aboard defies the imagination. Over thirty-seven tons of fresh meat; twelve tons of poultry and game; one and a quarter ton of sausages; over a ton of coffee; five tons of sugar; 36,000 oranges; a half ton of grapes; 1,500 gallons of milk; three tons of butter; seven thousand heads of lettuce; over two tons of tomatoes; forty tons of potatoes; 20,000 bottles of beer and stout; and 8,000 cigars.

Sailing day came early. Right after the sun rose amid fair skies the *Titanic*'s crew members began converging on the ship. They came in droves with sea bags and gear to settle in their quarters. There was boisterous commotion and celebration among the men because of their new employment and the meeting of old friends. Captain Edward John Smith boarded before 7:00 a.m. and proceeded at once to his quarters to check the sailing report from his chief officer Henry Tingle Wilde.

Regular watches had been kept through the night by the ship's officers who were attending to assignments covering all the odd and end details required on the final night before departure.

The Board of Trade Immigration Officer Maurice Harvey Clarke was aboard early too, monitoring and directing the crew muster and witnessing the lowering of two lifeboats supervised by Fifth Officer Lowe and Sixth Officer Moody. The exercise included the manning and lowering of starboard boats No. 11 and 15. With each boat containing a bo'sun and seven seamen, they were lowered away to the water, pulled around the dock, and hoisted back aboard. The half-hour drill, using only two lifeboats, with only two officers and fourteen crewmen participating, was over by 9:30 a.m.

This scant and bare minimum effort resulting in a lack of crucial lifeboat lowering, training, and supervision procedures, that should have been learned by all, would have serious repercussions in the days to come.

Thomas Andrews, the managing director of Harland and Wolff, who had arrived very early, seemed to be everywhere at once checking, addressing, and accomplishing last minute tests and inspections. Accompanying him was a staff of nine, who would work beside the ship's engineers to offer assistance in gaining valuable knowledge of the various systems underway.

Bruce Ismay, whose customary practice it was to sail on each new vessel's maiden voyage, came aboard around 9:30 a.m., with his wife, three children, a manservant, and secretary. His family, there to see him off, would not be joining him on the voyage.

Among the nearly three hundred second-class passengers who boarded, were eight members of the ships orchestra who would settle in to a cabin on E deck. Near their quarters was the cabin of Miss Edwina Celia Troutt, a twenty-seven-year-old lady travelling with two friends, Miss Suzie Webber and Miss Nora Keane. Lawrence Beesley, a science master at Dulwich College in London was coming to America for vacation. Before sailing, second-class passengers were allowed to tour all the first class surroundings, salons, and entertainment areas.

Under the scrutiny of a medical officer, hundreds of third-class passengers came aboard through an aft entrance on C deck. With a language barrier to hinder the embarking, the confused throng was ushered along by stewards who used gestures and loud broken phrases to herd the groups to their respective small cabins. A disorganized onslaught of wailing children, impatient adults, and short-tempered parents, prodded by the ship's crew, all filed through the maze of stairways and companionways to the lower reaches of steerage. In search of their surroundings some would wander through corridors and up stairways to finally reach the dead end, screened and locked, off-limit second class areas.

Many of the first class passengers, having arrived on a dockside train around 11:30 a.m., were coming aboard on B deck in such great numbers that the purser had great difficulty in maintaining his records. These guests were greeted by the chief steward and his staff, who directed and escorted them to their staterooms.

The who's-who list of passengers included such notables as the founder of Macy's department store, Mr. Isidor Straus, and his wife; distinguished author, Col. Archibald Gracie; Multi-millionaire, Mr. John J. Astor and his wife; renowned artist, Francis Millet; President Taft's military aide, Archibald Butt; President of Grand Trunk Railroad, Mr. C. M. Hays; Scotland's Countess of Rothes; and William T. Stead, editor of the *Review of Reviews*.

Close to fifty passengers had cancelled their reservations. Some were disenchanted with the location of their cabins. Others would miss the maiden voyage due to family or

business commitments. These passengers would undoubtedly become members of the "I almost sailed on the *Titanic*"
or the "Just Missed it Club".

According to an editorial in the April 19, 1912, Columbus (Ohio) Citizen, there were 3,478 Americans, 2,950
Britons, and 476 other would-be travellers from various coun-
tries who had cancelled their reservations before the *Titanic*
sailed. Today, there is the successor organization: the "My
grandparents almost sailed on the *Titanic* Club." Who knows
how many members these clubs have today? For certain a
vast number of those cancelled parties could count themselves
lucky, for if all the "just missed its" managed to embark on
the big ship she would have sunk at the Southampton dock!

As the pilot conferred with Captain Smith with regard to the low tide, the ship's thirty-nine foot depth, turning,
and the confining waterways ahead, the ship's officers were
dispatched to their stations and were standing ready to get
underway.

The electric spark of excitement was building. With
almost everyone aboard, the docks were filled with those to
see the *Titanic* off. Loved ones left behind, friends, and the
curious were beginning the last of the last goodbyes. Just
before noon, a great surge of white steam found its way to the
whistles as a resonant and hearty blast erupted and echoed
throughout the harbor to announce the coming departure. Two
more great bellows reverberated through the spring air.

Mooring lines came aboard and the tugs began gently
pulling the great lady clear of the dock. Ever so slowly, the
tugs guided her to the turning circle, an area where the dock
waters and the sea channel met. Tug hawsers were let go and
with precision and caution, her giant bulk was turned toward
the channel waters. An ever so slight tremor was felt throughout the ship as the bridge ordered all ahead slow.

Nearby, moored side by side, lay the steamers *Oce-
anic* and *New York*, idled by the coal strike. As *Titanic*'s great

displacement increased the water level surrounding these vessels, the *New York* was lifted so that her mooring lines slackened. Then as the *Titanic* passed, the volume of water beneath the *New York* was quickly sucked away leaving that vessel to porpoise violently. Snapping her mooring lines like thread, the *New York*'s stern was drawn toward the *Titanic*'s hull. The *New York* drifted broadside and dangerously close to the passing *Titanic*.

Captain Smith quickly perceived the eminent danger and ordered full astern to quickly check and halt his vessels forward movement. Fortunately on the second attempt, the tug *Vulcan* managed to get a line on the *New York* to stop that vessel within only a few feet of *Titanic*'s hull. With more lines on the *New York* she still drifted, but was brought under control, and then finally stopped. The mishap delayed the departure for nearly an hour, and it is imagined that those who lined the rails to witness the near calamity must have had uneasy feelings about this new vessel and the maiden voyage now beginning.

Chapter Five

To Cherbourg and Queenstown

There in splendor to take on more,
Through her gangways did they pour.
The rich and famous, what a show.
Lucky those who did not go.

The six hours of steaming across the seventy-seven mile breadth of the English Channel to Cherbourg, France offered passengers their first idea of the luxury, surroundings, and steadiness of the *Titanic*. With all of her lights already aglow, her anchor was dropped at 6:30 p.m. that evening of April 10, 1912. Impatient passengers, some grumbling over the delay of the new liner's arrival, were gathered to be brought to her side.

Since there were no docking facilities there to accommodate the big liners, the passengers coming aboard from this port had to be ferried to the *Titanic* aboard two specially-designed tenders built at Harland and Wolff for this purpose. The two-hundred and twenty foot *Nomadic* could carry up to one thousand first and second class passengers and the one hundred and seventy-five foot *Traffic*, also fitted with a conveyor system, could accommodate five hundred third class travelers. In addition, each tender could also carry the great abundance of luggage always associated with ocean travel. In bringing their "possibles" with them for the voyage, some passengers it seemed always went to the extreme. When Mr. and Mrs. Thomas Cardeza boarded at Cherbourg, they brought with them fourteen trunks, four suitcases and three crates of baggage. Mrs. Cardeza would later file a $177,352.75 claim for the loss of this luggage.

Included in the 142 first class passengers coming aboard was millionaire playboy, Mr. Benjamin Guggenheim, Sir Cosmo and Lady Duff Gordon, whose wife was the famous fashion designer Lucile; Mrs. James J. (Margaret) Brown, the "Unsinkable Molly" Brown; and Mr. Emil Brandeis, department store millionaire.

Of the thirty second class passengers, the noted American marine illustrator Samuel Ward Stanton embarked as well. There were one hundred and two third class travelers who filed aboard.   Saved from the awful fate that would follow, twenty-two passengers disembarked.   As those departing looked back, they were caught for a moment in breathless awe over the spectacular sight. Her immense stature, alight with countless specks of brightness pouring from all her portholes and sidelights, would be a sight they would never forget.

In port only ninety minutes, her anchor was drawn up, a careful reverse turn was ordered, and the liner was once again underway by 8:10 p.m. Soon the distant night lights of Cherbourg faded into the low mist on the horizon. The *Titanic,* now knifing the seas with unleashed and unrestrained power, raced along on her night leg to Queenstown, Ireland.

By this time the excitement had worn off for many of her passengers. Some had been electrified by their first ocean voyage, others were thrilled at being aboard on this maiden voyage, and some, accustomed to the luxury of ocean travel, seemed passive.

There was time to explore all the amenities and pleasures aboard for first class passengers. A dip in the swimming pool, a soothing Turkish bath, or a short respite in the new-fangled electric bath delighted many. A thirty by twenty-foot squash racket court was available too. Guests were charged four shillings ($1.00) for an electric or Turkish bath, one shilling ($.25) to swim if a Turkish bath was not booked, and two shillings ($.50) for use of the racket court. The gymnasium, having large windows with a grand view of the sea, attracted its share of the more athletic types.

The first and second-class libraries catered to those seeking a good book. Some found the barber shop or the clothes pressing room to primp for a special evening. There was a dark room for photography enthusiasts, and reading and writing rooms for those so inclined. Others found the relaxing but cool solitude in a deck chair wrapped in a blanket with a cup of evening tea. Lovers too were inspired at discovering the rapture of tender embraces by the rail on the romantic night.

Many guests were quite interested in the novelty of the passenger elevators, three of which accommodated those in first class. These roomy lifts saved the drudgery of climbing the many stairs and could travel a hundred feet per minute.

If walking was your pleasure, the ship's broad teak decks stretched for what seemed like miles, and could hone your appetite to the fullest measure. One might indulge in a game of cards, chess, checkers, or "horse racing in miniature," a betting contest using small horses and jockeys on a track laid out on the deck. You could easily find warm and friendly conversation in one of the smoking rooms. For the more energetic, a grand tour of the entire ship was suggested as an interesting activity designed to offset even the slightest hint of boredom.

As word of the notion got around, many travellers would be anxious to send "wish you were here" or "we're on the *Titanic*" wireless messages to friends and family back home.

While the third class areas were certainly less lavish than those in first or second class, they were by no means as sparse or cramped as they were aboard other vessels at the time. The general room with a piano, dining salon, open deck areas forward and aft, and for that matter, even the cabins were spacious, handsomely decorated, and comfortable for the cost of the fare.

All aboard would look forward to the very eloquent and fanciful tradition of summoning guests to dinner by the ship's bugler, P. W. Fletcher. For every meal, the neatly uniformed gent, offering his rendition of *The Roast Beef of Old England*, would invite passengers to another sumptous feast.

The highly appetizing meals served were perhaps the one feature that contributed to most everyone's enjoyment. Breakfast was served from 8:30 to 10:30, luncheon from 1:00 to 2:30, and dinner from 6:00 to 7:30. With the very best food obtainable, kept fresh in the vast stores, the exquisite cuisine was prepared by top chefs, offered in generous portions, and served by courteous and attentive stewards and stewardesses.

Accommodating five hundred and thirty-two passengers, the first-class dining salon and spacious reception room was the largest found on any liner of the period. Second-class dining equalled that of first class accommodations on most liners. This seventy-one foot salon extended the full width of the ship, and could seat three hundred and ninety-four people.

Exhausted from the anxious moments of hectic boarding, settling in, and touring their surroundings, many of the passengers had retired content in knowing they were safe and secure in their cabins. Meanwhile, work continued for stewards, bakers, pursers, and all those associated with keeping the ship operative and alive during its quiet hours. Labor for those in the bowels of the ship never ceased. The stokers were hard at it, feeding coal to the gaping furnaces for the steam required to service the vessel as she coursed along.

Through the night she sped onward back through the English Channel and northwest to Queenstown, again to feel the Atlantic's swell. By noon, April 11th, she had dropped anchor two miles offshore and was ready to receive passengers and mail.

The tenders *America* and *Ireland* would soon be at her side with one hundred and thirteen third class passengers and over thirteen hundred sacks of mail. Hidden among the mail bags along with those who disembarked was Stoker, John Coffey. When he signed on the *Titanic* he registered an address in Queenstown, and it was believed that he was simply after a free trip home.

Another stoker caused considerable alarm among some of the passengers just before departure. Taking a break from the searing surroundings near the boilers, this man found a way to catch a breath of fresh and cooling air. Climbing up the ladder inside the number four funnel, which was a dummy stack for ventilation purposes, he peered from the rim of the stack, having a splendid view from that vantage. His face, black with soot, was taken by a few to be that of the devil himself, an ominous and frightful premonition that would, for some, haunt the voyage.

The first of three resounding blasts brought the doomsayers back to reality as the reports announced that the time for departing was at hand. By 1:30 p.m., her starboard anchor was secured, and her great screws again churned the waters pushing her great mass past Roche's Point and onward. After one more quick stop to disembark her pilot she made a broad starboard turn, and passed a nearby trawler to which she answered a passing and farewell salute. Other than during a noon test of the whistles each day, it would be the last time her gigantic whistles would be heard.

Her name yet untarnished, she was at her best and in her glory, finally steaming westward in the Atlantic, coursing through the great domain in which she was intended for. To have seen her there as the golden sunset gave way to the coming darkness, with her lights all sparkling and her mass imposing and regal, would, no doubt have left one breathless.

Chapter Six

Her Days at Sea

Across the great expanse she flew,
Was she after the speed prize blue?
Twenty-four were lit that day,
Ignoring warnings along the way.

Having spent their first full day at sea, passengers had settled into a relaxing mode of shipboard content. At noon each day, those interested could monitor the progress of the passage by checking the number of miles travelled. This information was posted in the smoking rooms. By the first posting that Friday, the 12th of April, the ship had steamed 386 miles. Less than expected by those without any sea knowledge, but she was just getting into it, gradually coming up to the speed she was designed for. There was conjecture too, because word was already about that she would be after a speed record. This, mind you, was a "galley wireless" rumor, not anything officially declared by the ship's officers. However, everyone knew what the big liners and their owners were after—that illustrious Atlantic speed prize. Reportedly, considerable difficulties would have arisen for the White Star Line had the *Titanic* raced for a record crossing. This, according to company officials, would have caused her to arrive early and at night, when docking the ship would have been extremely difficult. However, crossing records were generally figured from pilot to pilot, excluding the time involved in departing and docking on each end of a voyage. So she still could have been racing for that mark (pilot) off New York with intent to anchor until daylight or until she could have been received with a glorious welcome.

Contrary to what might be expected on the maiden voyage of the biggest, grandest ocean liner ever built, there were no gala parties, elegant captain's balls, or special dinners. Aside from not having any of the ceremonies already mentioned, there was not even a maiden voyage ball or even the most low-key social affair to celebrate her coming out.

Captain Smith, following that conservative standard, did not dine or socialize with notables and celebrities either. He sat at his usual table for six in the first-class dining salon, or if inclement weather dictated, he dined in his quarters or on the bridge.

Without an activities director aboard, passengers were left to find their own amusement and pleasure. The *Titanic*'s maiden voyage then, as seen from the perspective of the passenger, was one for quiet and relaxation, each party or small group off by themselves, savoring and enjoying the passage.

Second-class passenger Lawrence Beesley found himself quite at home, intensely interested in every detail of the voyage. He closely observed how the ship was run, examining the various parts of the vessel open to him, and followed the ship's course with more than a passing interest. This kept him fairly busy, yet his interest in reading a good book gave him ample quiet time as well.

Thomas Andrews and his group were not on holiday. They were continuously gauging the performance of all the ship's systems and documenting and advising how to improve operation. After all, not only was it break-in time for all the equipment on the new ship, but all the engineers, chiefs, and officers required attention too. Considerable time and effort was necessary to work up to a level of proficiency in order to exact the best operational standard from the propulsion system and all the other gear as well.

At 10:30 each morning Captain Smith would lead an inspection team throughout the entire ship. Accompanied by the chief engineer, chief steward, surgeon, and the purser and his assistant, the group toured galleys, storerooms, dispensaries, shops, saloons, cargo holds, and all public areas in all classes. Then he and the chief engineer would tour and inspect the engine rooms and all the deck gear. It was a time to scrutinize crew performance, area cleanliness, and equipment operation to document potential problem areas and note possible improvements,

Following this inspection, Smith would convene with his top officers, discuss the results of the tour, make appropriate changes, issue associated orders, and review the navigation details of the day.

There were still a lot of passengers wanting to send wireless messages. At the inquiry office near the first-class entrance, passengers paid 12 shillings 6 pence ($3.15 US) for the first ten words and 9 pence (22.5¢ US) for each word thereafter. From there messages flew via pneumatic tube to the wireless shack where the wireless operator read and sent the message.

Messages received were typed on a Marconi form, then transferred back through pneumatic tubes to the inquiry desk by the receiving operators. Incoming ship's business, or navigational messages were delivered directly to the bridge which was just a short distance away.

Numerous congratulatory messages had been received by Friday morning and along with some of them came the first ice advisories. Messages from the *Empress of Britain* bound from Halifax to Liverpool and the *La Touraine* from New York to Le Havre, both included information about ice conditions.

Even though ice was expected along that course in April, it was probably not known at the time that vessels arriving and departing western north Atlantic ports reported more drift ice farther south than in some years. Ice fields had extended far down into the southern track. Some vessels reported being completely shut in by ice fields for as far as they could see, extending to the horizon in every direction. Sightings of icebergs with sixty to one hundred foot walls with spires reaching heights of two-hundred and fifty feet were not unusual.

By noon Saturday, April 13th, the *Titanic* had travelled nine hundred and five miles, covering five hundred and nineteen miles in the previous twenty-four hours. Now she was dashing through the smooth seas in a spectacle of grace and splendor. She had registered one hundred and thirty-three more miles than in the previous twenty-four hour period.

Ice warnings continued to pour in between the flood of messages outbound. Except for the hearty, the chill of the wind across her decks kept most passengers inside. The sliding window enclosures on the promenade deck was proven to have been worth the last-minute effort, as guests could walk there protected from the cold breeze. The hours passed quickly as friends gathered in the great rooms for games, dining, or warm conversation.

Concerts by the ship's orchestra were a popular and well-attended occasion. The talented musicians, divided into two groups, offered both first and second-class passengers pleasant listening in reception rooms, dining salons, and luncheon areas. Strolling musicians added a romantic touch to the dining room ambiance. They were professionals, each of them able to play from memory every song of the three-hundred and fifty-two titles in the White Star song book.

Second-class passenger Edwina Troutt's friend Nora Keane presented an aggravating predicament to disrupt her enjoyment of the crossing. From the time of boarding she had declared over and over that she felt the ship would never reach New York. This fear was exacerbated when she discovered that an acquaintance she had met earlier had heard a cock crowing one evening, an ominous omen for the superstitious aboard a vessel.

As it turned out, she probably did hear a rooster. Hens and roosters owned by a Mrs. J. Stuart White were being shipped in crates and stored near the dog kennels on F deck, well within hearing range of the lady who heard them.

The only time steerage passengers were allowed into any first-class area was for religious services. Humbly they filed into the luxury of the first-class dining salon with jaws dropped and eyes wide with amazement over the grandeur of the surroundings.

It was 10:30 a.m., Sunday, April 14th and Divine services were being conducted and led by Captain Smith. All joined in the hymns which were accompanied by the ship's orchestra and selected from the White Star Line prayer book.

At noon her great whistles bellowed for the final time in a test required by company regulation. They echoed far across the Atlantic's gentle swells in a lamenting and almost sorrowful drone.

According to the latest posting, the *Titanic* had sped five hundred and forty-six miles in the previous twenty-four hours.

First class passengers were enjoying an exquisite spread with such entrees as salmon, filet mignons lili, lamb, roast duckling, sirloin of beef or roast squab. If they dared indulge after their meal, for dessert there was waldorf pudding, peaches in chartreuse jelly, chocolate and vanilla eclairs, or French ice cream.

Second class passengers feasted on baked haddock, curried chicken, spring lamb, or roast turkey. Their desserts were no less sumptuous. There was plum pudding, coconut sandwiches, American ice cream, fresh fruit, and assorted nuts.

Third class passenger dinners, while certainly not comparable to the upper class menus, were none the less generous and filling. These dinners consisted of vegetable soup, roast pork, green peas, boiled potatoes, cabin biscuits, fresh bread, plum pudding, and oranges.

More ice warnings came in from the steamer *Caronia* bound from New York to Liverpool. This message was sent to the bridge and was posted there by Captain Smith for his officers to note. It contained information from other westbound steamers that had reported icebergs, growlers, and field ice in 42° N., from 49° to 51° W. on April 12th.

A message sent to the United States Hydrographic office in Washington, D. C. from the liner *Amerika* reported the sighting of two large icebergs in 41° 27' N, 50°8' W on Sunday, April 14th. This message was relayed to the *Titanic,* but for some unknown reason it never reached the bridge.

From records prepared by the Hydrographic Office and revealed in the 62nd Congressional Senate inquiry investigating the causes of the disaster, no fewer than nine vessels, reported a proliferation of icebergs, growlers, and pack ice all sighted on April 14th, in the area the *Titanic* was steaming into.

Around 8:30 a large group of passengers gathered in the second-class saloon to sing hymns. Lawrence Beesley, anxious to take part in another facet of his voyage, was there to join in what seemed a fitting and spiritual end of that Sunday's activities.

Chapter Seven

Her Last Hours

She lifted high with lights aglow,
Strangely beautiful in the floe.
And as they clung to the ship with fright,
She slowly sank on that starry night.

With a noted drop in temperature, the chief engineer and the ship's carpenter were ordered to check the fresh water stores over concern that they might freeze. It was 8:40 p.m., and Second Officer Lightoller on duty on the bridge was having a brief conversation with Captain Smith about the weather. They were discussing the difficulty in spotting an iceberg under the prevailing conditions. Being that the sea was dead calm with hardly any wind, there would be very little sea action breaking against the base of an iceberg to offer visible detection.

As Captain Smith left the bridge, he advised Lightoller to notify him should any doubtful situation arise. Shortly thereafter, Lightoller alerted the lookouts to keep an extra sharp eye out for small ice and growlers. A growler, or small iceberg, could be as large as a three-bedroom house.

Meanwhile, the steamer *Mesaba* at a position north of the *Titanic,* reported heavy pack ice, field ice, and a number of large bergs at 9:40 p.m. The message was received by *Titanic*'s wireless operator, but again the message failed to reach the bridge.

First officer Murdoch relieved Lightoller on the bridge at 10:00 p.m., and lookouts Fleet and Lee took over that duty in the crow's nest. Word was passed to keep a sharp lookout for ice and growlers.

Around 10:30 p.m., a Morse signal lamp message was received from the freighter *Rappahannock,* which was eastbound from Halifax and close enough to see *Titanic*'s lights. The *Rappahannock* had sustained rudder damage after passing through an immense and heavy ice field containing several icebergs. The message was acknowledged by *Titanic.*

Without reducing her speed, in the face of the surrounding and eminent danger of icebergs, the *Titanic* raced onward with twenty-four of her twenty-nine boilers lit at twenty-two and a half knots - nearly twenty-six mph.

In regard to what was about to happen to the *Titanic,* the incident involving the message sent by the freighter *Californian* was perhaps the most appalling. The *Californian* was surrounded by ice and was contacting all vessels in the area with that information. The *Titanic*'s operator took the message around 10:55 p.m., but then abruptly cut it off half way through with a rude, "Keep out! Shut up! You're jamming my signal. I'm working Cape Race." The wireless operator was swamped because many of *Titanic*'s affluent passengers were sending "wish you were here" messages to friends boasting about the grand time they were having on the new ship.

The final moments on the grand vessel, still unblemished by the disaster that would soon associate her with maritime tragedy forever, passed quickly.

The air was bitterly cold, the night profoundly clear, and the sea was calm and flat as a mill pond. It was so calm, in fact, that stars low on the horizon were distinctly reflected in the sea. Then at 11:30 p.m., the *Titanic* steamed into a very slight haze, which created even more of a difficulty for the lookouts who peered into the blackness ahead.

Because of his honed reflexes, lookout Fleet, with a sudden almost instinctive flash of movement, gave three sharp rings on the warning bell to indicate "object directly ahead." He then grabbed the telephone and frantically rang for the bridge.

"Yes, What do you see?"

"Iceberg right ahead."

The iceberg materialized from the mist as a giant black mass right off the bow. As the *Titanic* swung to port, the lookouts tensed for an impact that never came. They watched in awe as the berg moved past along the starboard side still enveloped in the slight mist which was now illuminated by the lights on the ship. Expecting more of a crash, they heard nothing save the sound of shaved off chunks of ice hitting the well deck area. Gathering their thoughts, they realized that in the absence of any pronounced impact or sound, the frightening encounter was probably nothing more than a close call.

As a junior officer on the bridge acknowledged the message, Murdoch quickly moved to order engines stopped and reversed on the telegraph. In the same instant he ordered quartermaster Robert Hichens to "hard-a-starboard," and the wheel was quickly spun hard over as far as it would travel.

Murdoch's next action was to quickly review instructions for closing the watertight doors, before actuating the lever to electrically move the doors closed. This procedure, it seems, should have been familiar to a top officer on the new ship. It was another procedure or routine that would have been rehearsed at length during more thorough sea trials.

As the *Titanic* slowly swung to port, contact was made with what was thought to have been an underwater spur of the berg. It was 11:40 p.m.

Down below in Boiler room No. 6, Fireman Frederick Barrett was shocked to see sea water explode through the wall of the compartment above the floor plating. The berg had opened the hull with random gashes and punctures for 249 feet from Hold No. 1 all the way back to a few feet into Boiler Room No. 5.

Fourth officer Boxhall, upon hearing the warning bells, made his way to the bridge where he met Captain Smith who was asking Murdoch, "What have we struck?"

"An iceberg, Sir."

Murdoch explained that he had ordered the ship turned hard to port and reversed the engines, intending to then turn hard to starboard around the berg, but it was too close. He also informed Smith that he had closed the watertight doors. By this time the iceberg had vanished into the darkness astern.

Lawrence Beesley, snug in his cabin reading felt merely an extra jiggle of his mattress. Shortly thereafter he felt the same sensation again. He thought that perhaps the engines had just increased their speed, but a few moments later he felt them slow and then stop. Other passengers did not feel much more.

Some heard a grinding or scraping sound most likely made by the iceberg as it passed along the starboard side. Of course, most passengers had retired for the night, unaware of what had taken place.

Captain Smith directed Boxhall to go below to examine the forward areas of the ship and report back to the bridge as soon as possible. As Boxhall left the bridge, he noticed Captain Smith moving the telegraph handles to "half ahead."

In his cabin, still deeply engrossed in his work, Thomas Andrews hadn't noticed anything unusual, not even the stoppage of the engines. His study was interrupted with word that he was wanted on the bridge. Once there, he and Captain Smith proceeded to tour the forward areas of the ship via crew corridors and accesses so as not to frighten any passengers.

Fireman Frederick Barrett had already abandoned Boiler Room No. 6 as it was completely flooded. Water was steadily rising, filling the first five compartments, and gradually pulling the ship down at the bow.

Bruce Ismay, asleep in his suite on B deck was awakened by a scraping sound. With thoughts that perhaps the ship had lost a propeller blade, he stepped into the corridor and encountered a steward who could offer no definitive information.

Now with an overcoat over his night-clothes he went to the bridge where he asked Captain Smith what had happened.

"We have struck ice," Smith responded.

"Is the ship seriously damaged?" queried Ismay.

"I am afraid she is."

Returning to his cabin Ismay met Chief Engineer Bell whom he asked the same question. Bell also said the ship was gravely damaged but assured Ismay that the pumps should certainly keep the vessel afloat.

Beesley and a few other passengers had ventured up on deck seeking a cause of the delay. It was about 12:15 a.m. and Beesley saw that the ship had already resumed her course. He also noticed a lifeboat being uncovered in a manner that appeared to be just a precautionary measure.

Some of the passengers had picked up pieces of the iceberg strewn on the deck. They were amazed at the novelty of the event that offered them such a strange souvenir.

Passenger Edwina Troutt also on deck in the bitter cold asked the purser what was wrong. "We've just stopped for a while but we're moving on again," he told her.

No alarm had been sounded. Because there was no official word of any danger, many crewmen and passengers alike had no idea what was going on. This on one hand caused considerable confusion, but the shortage of information at least helped to prevent hysteria.

After their sounding inspection below, Captain Smith and Thomas Andrews conferred on the findings. Explaining that as the bow sank lower and lower, the water in Boiler Room No. 6 would flow into number 5 to lower the bow more. This would cause water to flow into number 4, and eventually numbers 3 and 2.

Because the bulkheads (walls) between the lower compartments did not go up to the top of each compartment, the water could flow freely from one compartment to the next as the ship sank at the bow. The incoming sea water thereby filled and then cascaded on to the next compartment, and the next, until they all filled.

Andrews' staggering and terse announcement would stun all within earshot: "The ship is doomed."

Smith grimly asked the question he did not want to hear a response to.

"How long do we have?"

After a few calculations, Thomas responded, "An hour and a half. Possibly two. Not much longer"

Smith next ordered the uncovering of the lifeboats.

The *Titanic*'s position—41° 6' N, 50° 14' W—had already been worked out by Boxhall. Because of a possible failure to account for a one-knot southerly current, and possible failure to set the ship's clocks back to compensate for westward travel, along with an incorrect gauging of the ship's speed, Boxhall's estimate could have been off by four miles to the south and six miles east of the position which he gave.

Captain Smith took the co-ordinates to the wireless room and advised the operators to stand by to send a call for assistance. He returned a short while later with an order to send out a CDQ . . .CDQ . . . call for assistance.

How ironic. Just a short while before, the *Titanic* wireless operator had vehemently refused incoming navigational messages and now they were sending out a plea for help to the same vessels from which those messages had come.

Calm confusion reigned. Many passengers were still asleep; some were headed back to their warm beds. Many were told that everything was fine. Card games were still being played in the first-class smoking room, the band was playing merry music in the lounge, while others were advised to don a lifebelt because, "you may need it later."

Third-class passengers, being in the lower parts of the ship, were awakened by a jar. They needed no official word, for stark evidence of something dreadfully wrong came in the form of water rushing into their quarters.

Immediately they began to move away from the water toward the stern. With ragged suitcases and odd-looking bundles, most of them were carrying everything they owned. There was more of a sense of fear among them too, unlike the relative calm of their first and second-class counterparts.

Soon hundreds of them were gathered in the aft well deck and on the poop deck, as far away as they could get from the obvious bow-down dilemma.

Second-class passengers Jacob Milling and Edgar Andrew joked about the directive a crewman shouted as he walked through the hallway. "All passengers put your lifebelts on and go up on top deck. Leave everything. It is only a precaution and you can return to your cabins."

Small groups of men began to unfasten lifeboat covers. After convincing some frightened ladies that the ship indeed was moving on again, Beesley returned to his cabin again to read for a while after which he heard the command, "All passengers on deck with life belts on."

At 12:45 a.m. the ship had stopped for good, lying motionless on the calm sea.

Quartermaster George Rowe began firing distress rockets that shot some eight hundred feet high into the night and exploded into a shower of bright stars. This was enough to unnerve and bring alarming questions to the minds of those who had been so calm before. Added to that ominous sight was the deafening roar of steam being released from the fore and aft exhaust ports on all four stacks. It was difficult to hear even shouted directives.

It was around this time that Officer Boxhall observed a vessel approaching at a distance of five or six miles. With his naked eye he saw the green and red side lights of the approaching ship. Soon after he noticed only the vessel's red side light and masthead lights. Along with Quartermaster

Rowe, he attempted to signal the vessel with the Morse lamp, but the vessel steamed away into the night without acknowledging the message.

At 12:45 a.m., overseen by Officer Murdoch, Boat No. 7, the first boat was lowered and the first on the starboard side was sent down with only twenty-eight people aboard. The boat was lowered to the rail so that others could board, then lowered to the gangway to await further orders or other occupants.

This boat could have held sixty-five people. It is true that there was difficulty finding women and children to fill the boats, but there was no procedure either. There hadn't been any boat drills or any guidelines to direct passengers to a particular lifeboat in case of emergency. Moreover, there was uncertainty as to the total capacity of the boats. Unbeknown to *Titanic*'s officers, and later revealed in the British inquiry, the lifeboats, using the new Welin davits, had been lowered in a test at the shipyard with a full capacity of people. This very important bit of knowledge should have been made known during sea trials.

Most everyone knew by this time to proceed to the boat deck because there was eminent danger. And yet there were many who refused to accept that reality. Many would not believe the vessel would actually sink.

First-class passenger Mrs.Isidor Straus was approached and asked if she would like to get in a lifeboat, to which she emphatically responded, "No!"

At 12:55 a.m., Boat No. 5 on the starboard side and Boat No. 6 on the port side were lowered.

Boat No. 5, with forty-one people, was lowered with great difficulty. Several times one end of the boat or the other was lowered faster than the opposite end, adding additional horror to the nightmare. Among the boat's occupants were ten male passengers, Third Office Pitman, and four crewmen, one stewardess, and two other men. A German, Doctor

Frauenthal, and Isaac P. Mauge jumped into the boat as it was being sent down.

Boat No. 6 held twenty-eight people. Among these was first-class passenger Molly Brown, who was forcefully put into the boat. Three crewmen, one boy with an injured arm, and Major A. G. Peuchen were also in the boat.

At 1:00 a.m., Boat No. 3 on the starboard side was lowered. This boat contained fifty people made up of twenty-five women and children, ten male passengers, and fifteen crewmen. It was said that no other women were around that area to be loaded. A call was sent out for more women and when none came forward, men were allowed to get in the boat.

At 1:10 a.m., Emergency Boat No. 1 on the starboard side and Boat No. 8. on the port side were lowered. Able to hold forty people, Boat No. 1 contained a total of twelve people which included two women: Lady Duff Gordon and her maid Miss Francatelli; five men including Lord Duff Gordon and seven crewmen. No other women were in the area.

Boat No. 8 contained twenty-four women and four crewmen. No male passengers were in this boat. Pulling for what they thought were lights of a ship in the distance, they rowed for hours, never coming any closer to those lights. At the tiller was Lucy Noel Martha, Countess of Rothes.

At 1:20 a.m., Boat No. 10 on the port side and Boat No. 9 on the starboard side were lowered. Boat No. 10 had no male passengers, but had forty-one women, seven children, five crewmen, one Japanese stowaway, and one Armenian man who jumped into the boat from A deck as it was being lowered.

Boat No. 9 was sent down with a total of sixty-three aboard. This included two or three men, eight to ten crewmen and women from first, second and third-class.

A considerable list to port now effected the loading of

the boats. An elderly lady, attempting to cross the gap between the rail and the boat fell and was badly injured. The wife of author Jacques Futrelle was physically forced into the boat.

More rockets shot skyward, again reminding all of their foreboding meaning. Finally the stark realization hit hard. Many more passengers would have to be put into each boat.

At 1:25 a.m., two boats were lowered, Boat No. 11 on the starboard side and Boat No. 12 on the port side.

Boat No. 11 was lowered into the path of a great stream of water gushing from the side of the ship. The boat had to be kept clear of the discharge. The boat held seventy passengers in all. Mostly containing women (including one stewardess) and children, there were also three male passengers and eight crewmen.

Boat No. 12 contained a total of forty-three people. Of these there were forty women and children and a single French male passenger who jumped into the boat as it was going down. The man hid in the lower parts of the boat and could not be found. The remainder were crewmen, some of whom were later transferred from another boat.

Some of the boats in the water rowed away into the darkness, while others remained stationary a short distance away. With a megaphone, Captain Smith hailed the boats several times with orders to return for more people, but no boats returned.

Thomas Andrews was shocked at the number of women who refused to board lifeboats. He went here and there pleading, "There is little time left, you must get into the boats!"

The sight of rising water covering the E deck landing could be seen at the bottom of the winding staircase as first-class passengers ascended the stairs on the way topside. If it hadn't dawned on them before, the frightful sight of the sea bubbling up in plain view below was enough to convince them of the impending disaster.

To some of those in boats on the water who watched the remaining boats being lowered, the scene was hard to comprehend. The bow of the great ship was sinking lower and lower by the minute, inevitable catastrophe was approaching, yet passengers held back in small groups seemingly unconcerned. Those who were boarding the boats did so without panic as if they were getting into a canoe for a Sunday picnic.

Tearful good-bye kisses and last tender embraces punctuated by the strains of the band playing soft music on the slanting deck made for a heart-wrenching scene.

At 1:30 a.m., Boat No. 14 was lowered on the port side. This boat would have sixty occupants including fifty women, six crewmen, and four men who were later pulled from the sea. There was also one Italian man who came aboard the boat with a shawl over his head appearing as a woman.

There was difficulty in lowering this boat too. There was fear that the boat would separate from the load. Officer Lowe, in command of the boat, fired three gun shots into the air when it appeared that scores of men from steerage might jump into the boat. They were lining the rails and gaping at those in the boat.

At 1:35 a.m., Boats No. 13 and No. 15 on the starboard side and No. 16 on the port side were lowered.

In a strange coincidence Boat No 13 contained three of the main players in this book: Second-class passengers Edwina Troutt and Lawrence Beesley, and Fireman Frederick Barrett. In all, the boat held sixty-four people including four male passengers and several crewmen.

The vessel was down at the bow at a severe enough angle to reveal her giant propellers. To the people boarding the after-most boats, the distance to the water below was a most terrifying height.

As Boat No. 13 was being loaded, a Peruvian man approached the area with a baby in his arms. One of the officers there stopped him in his tracks by shouting, "Stand back, English. . . .English!" It was an obvious attempt to keep a steerage passenger from entering a lifeboat.

The man with the baby pleaded, "I do not want to be saved, but please save this baby." The baby was then taken and placed in the arms of Edwina Troutt.

One of the last sights Miss Troutt had before being lowered away was that of people kneeling in prayer before a priest.

Sent down in the direct path of a three-foot diameter gush of condenser exhaust water pouring from the side of the ship, it was necessary to push the boat away from the hull with oars to avoid being filled with water. Because the boat was leaning against the hull due to the port list, it bumped and jarred along the rivets as it was lowered.

Boat No.16, lowered from the port side, contained fifty-six people, all women passengers except for one stewardess. There were no male occupants except for the five crewmen.

According to Steward C. E. Andrews who was later interrogated in the American Inquiry, although no male steerage passengers attempted to get in the boat he was in, he was told by an officer not to allow any to enter.

Boat No. 15 would be lowered containing seventy occupants. This would include fifty-three third-class women and children, one first-class man, three third-class men, and thirteen crewmen. Scouts were sent around in search for more women to board the boat. They found none.

The boat was lowered directly on top of Boat No. 13 on the water below. Through frantic pleas Boat No. 15 was finally stopped just a few feet above the boat beneath it.

At 1:40 a.m., the Engelhardt collapsible Boat C was lowered on the starboard side scraping along on the rivets as it went down. Of the thirty-nine occupants, there were five crewmen and Bruce Ismay. Four Orientals from steerage were discovered in the boat soon after dawn broke. They had hidden there between the seats. The rest of the occupants were women and children.

Chief Officer Wilde who oversaw the lowering of that boat asked if there were any women and children to board. None came forth so Mr. Ismay went into the boat.

The sea had now reached the very top of the forepeak. As high and mighty as the proud vessel once stood, she was now humbled and insulted by the ever-rising sea.

At this time, if you had ventured as far forward toward the bow as you could, past her great bow anchor, and put your hand on the bulwark there, your fingers would have been touching sea water. (See bow view of the sinking *Titanic* at 1:40 a.m., April 15, 1912 on back cover)

At 1:45 a.m., Emergency Boat No. 2, with a total of twenty-five people was lowered without any rush of passengers to get in the boat. However, sixteen or eighteen stokers filed into the boat and were quickly chastised and sent out. The boat contained one third-class elderly man, three crewmen including Fourth Officer Boxhall, and twenty-one women and children.

There was difficulty in getting the boat free from its lines, which had to be cut with a knife.

Approximately fifty-eight miles away, the Cunarder *Carpathia* had received *Titanic*'s grim pleas for help and had immediately set a course to rendezvous with the stricken liner. She would spend several hours speeding through ice fields herself before she could reach the scene. Could the life of the great ship be extended until the *Carpathia* arrived to render aid?

At 1:55 a.m., Boat No. 4 was lowered from the port side. There were no male passengers in this boat, which contained thirty-six women and children and four crewmen.

Several other crewmen were picked up out of the water.

Steward A. Cunningham waited until all the boats had left. He then jumped into the water and swam like a champion away from the ship nearly three-quarters of a mile, afraid that he might be drawn down when the vessel sank. In the water a half-hour he heard voices from a lifeboat, hailed the boat, and was pulled from the sea. Siebert, another sailor was also picked up, but died in the boat.

Not only women from first and second-class refused to leave the ship. Many women in third-class would not leave their husbands or families as well. While women were allowed access to the boat deck, the third class men were not. Because the gates to the second class areas were locked, access to this area from the aft well deck was impossible. This resulted in some of the men having to climb the cranes there in order to ascend to the upper decks. No wonder less than a quarter of those in steerage would be saved.

At 2:05 a.m., the Engelhardt collapsible Boat D was sent down with forty-four occupants including forty women and children, two crewmen, and two male passengers. It was the last boat to be lowered. Once again there was a call for women to board, and none came. But when several men began to climb into the boat, some women were brought forward, so the men in the boat got out without any hesitation or trouble.

Shouted pleas with a megaphone went unanswered again as those in lifeboats stood off refusing to return to take more passengers. There were arguments in the boats between crewmen and passengers over whether or not to return to take more passengers.

Around 2:10 a.m., the bow plunged beneath the sea, causing a rush of water to envelop the bridge and officer quarters.

Many of those on deck were washed off by the approaching wave and engulfed in the cold water. Others unable to maintain footing on the slanting deck slid helplessly into the sea as well.

Many stories abound concerning Captain Smith's last actions as the *Titanic* sank. Lightoller being within sight of him and honorably on duty to the last moment relates that after the captain had done all that he could, he turned and dove into the sea.

The last two boats to leave the *Titanic* were not launched, but were floated off as the rising sea set them adrift. These were two Engelhardt collapsibles A and B that were attached to the roof of the officers' house.

In the words of Second Officer Lightoller being questioned in the Senate Inquiry, "There was nothing more to be done."

When asked, "Did you leave the ship?"

Lightoller replied, "No, the ship left me."

He was therefore serving passengers and gallantly doing his duty to the very last. In doing so he became a victim to one of the most harrowing incidents involved with the sinking.

After diving head first into the chilled sea, he was quickly pulled back on the grating over an air vent that fed ventilation to the stoke hole. He was sucked against this grating as the ship was sinking, with the heavy sea pouring over and holding him fast in this absolute nightmarish position. Suddenly, there was a saving and terrific blast of air or great bubble that was blown from below to set him free. Managing to escape but a few feet from the suction, he was sucked back once again in the same manner, but was finally released in the same way.

Col. Archibald Gracie was sucked down by the same horror as sea water rushed by him as the ship was sinking.

As the stern rose higher into the air the number one funnel fell creating a great splash that washed Lightoller and others struggling nearby a good distance from the sinking ship. He clung with others to the overturned boat until picked up by the *Carpathia*.

Burned in their memory, those who witnessed those final moments of the great *Titanic* could never erase the horrible sight. Bruce Ismay turned away, unable to look at the death of his dream.

Rising nearly erect with her lights still aglow she presented a spectacular yet horrifying scene. The roar of hundreds of screaming victims was only masked by the sound of tremendous crashing and clamor. Some of those left aboard found footing on the walls of deckhouses. Others were crammed into the well deck area or clinging to railings waiting for the sea to reach them. Hoping to enter the water and swim away from the feared suction, some jumped from the great height at the stern to sustain severe injury from the plunge.

When all at once her lights went out those staring at her brightness were robbed of their night vision and momentarily blinded in the total darkness. Settling back to about seventy degrees, she gradually gained speed until she sank beneath the sea. It was 2:20 a.m.

OF TITANIC

<u>Chapter Eight</u>

Too Late the Carpathia

Haunting screams heard year after year,
One boat returned 'cause of the fear.
So many helpless - only saved a few,
Sure to be swamped - what would you do?

"My heart went to my stomach and my stomach wasn't there." Those were the words uttered by ninety-seven-year-old survivor, Edwina Troutt McKenzie when asked what she felt upon seeing the *Titanic* sink. The screams of those left to die in the icy sea would echo within her until she died.

The sea, still calm, offered no sound to muffle the shouted pleas for help. Unable to mount the courage to go to them and render aid, all but a few of those in lifeboats surrounding the sinking stayed away fearing they would be swamped. It was this act of refusing aid to their fellow-man, more than the screams, that would haunt those that could have helped.

The Countess of Rothes in Lifeboat No. 8 urged a return, but was overruled by others. Some of those in Boat No. 6 were willing to go back as well, but they too were convinced by a crew member that they would be swamped.

Others weakly rationalized that if they could reach the ship whose lights they were rowing to, they could return with that ship to help others.

Under the charge of Quartermaster Perkis, only one boat, Boat No. 4 came back to the scene to render aid. Five crewmen were pulled aboard.

And so, one thousand, five hundred and seventeen

lives were lost, and only seven hundred and six people were saved. At least four hundred and seventy-three more could have found space in the lifeboats. This shameful situation which resulted from the lack of lifeboat drills and procedure, was compounded by the fear of many to even board a lifeboat. To think that there were not enough lifeboats for everyone aboard, yet the boats that left were not filled to capacity. At least the one hundred and fifty-seven women and children who were lost could have been saved.

The fear of boarding the lifeboats could have been averted or certainly eased had there been boat drills to help passengers overcome that fright. And if those in charge of lowering the boats had been sufficiently trained to lower them properly in an emergency situation, this too might have calmed the fears of those asked to board the boats. Those deciding whether or not to enter a lifeboat certainly must have been apprehensive enough without having to witness the haphazard way the boats were sent down.

Under the command of Captain Arthur Henry Rostron, the five-hundred and forty-foot Cunard liner *Carpathia* was bound from New York to the warmth of the Mediterranean. Designed for a total capacity of 2,550, she had only 743 passengers aboard and had departed her New York pier at noon on April 11, 1912.

Her single wireless operator, Harrold Cottam, had been on duty over seventeen hours when he received the frantic distress message from the sinking *Titanic*. He was about to turn in for the night, when he decided to send one more message. It was an advisory to the *Titanic* operator with word that there were several messages coming to him from Cape Cod.

During this transmission *Titanic* broke in: "Come at once. We have struck an iceberg. It's CQD, old man. Position 41° 46' N, 50° 14" W."

Carpathia: "Should I tell my Captain? Do you require assistance?"

Titanic: "Yes. Come quick."

Jolted fully awake from his weariness, Cottam dashed to the bridge, related the message to the duty officer, and within moments they both burst into Captain Rostron's quarters. The captain had just settled in bed and was angered over the abrupt and excited intrusion. After questioning the certainty of the message, Rostron sprang into action.

Quickly dressing, Rostron went directly to the chart room and began pouring over the chart which gave him his ship's position in relation to the *Titanic* according to her distress message. A distance of fifty-eight miles was calculated and the *Carpathia*'s course was immediately changed to North 52° West which would bring her to *Titanic*'s given position.

Rostron's sea experience and dedication guided him in formulating a heroic plan to utilize everything possible he had at his disposal to prepare for the rescue.

First he ordered *Carpathia*'s lifeboats to be made ready. He then called for his chief engineer and directed him to call extra stokers to duty. The ship's normal speed was fourteen-and-a-half knots, but she would soon be racing at over seventeen knots for the emergency situation.

He next called and advised the three ship's doctors and directed them to be situated at three appropriate locations to care for those coming aboard.

He summoned his officers to inform them as to what specific duties were necessary to handle the effort. There was wide-eyed shock when they learned that it was the *Titanic* they were rushing to. The chief steward and purser were to assign their men at the gangways to assist the survivors as they boarded.

All hands were mustered and served coffee. The stewards then prepared large amounts of hot drinks and soup for the expected survivors. All public rooms, officers' quarters, and even Captain Rostron's cabin were made ready. Those in steerage would be given a section in third class and their berths would be made ready for *Titanic*'s steerage. Expecting that the *Titanic* would have carried a great number of passengers, they did not know that so few of that number would actually board.

To hoist the injured or the children, chair slings and canvas bags were fashioned and placed at each gangway along with bright lights to illuminate the work. Ladders and lines were made ready to be slung over the side for those who could climb from the boats and large containers of oil were readied to pour down the forward heads to quiet the seas around the ship.

As *Carpathia*'s engines strained and the vibrations reverberated throughout the ship, passengers were awakened sensing something unusual. There was a beehive of crew activity in the corridors, yet it was in the middle of the night. While many sought answers as to the cause of the commotion, they were not told what was taking place. Instead they were assured that nothing was wrong and politley asked to stay in their cabins.

The wireless operator sent more intercepted messages to the bridge and the news was grim. Pleas from the *Titanic* told of her sinking by the bow, that women and children were being put off in lifeboats, and to come as soon as possible. The last message heard was that her engine room was flooded up to the boilers.

Onward she sped through the clear night on her gallant mission. Even though her lookouts would spot many large icebergs which required course changes to avoid them, she did not check her speed, bent on the urgency of the task.

Around 2:30 a.m. a single green flare was spotted off the bow a great distance away, and shortly thereafter Captain Rostron had rockets fired every fifteen minutes to let survivors know that help would soon be there.

At 3:35 a.m. the *Carpathia* was approaching the spot

where the *Titanic* should have been but nothing was seen. Soon faint green lights low on the sea were spotted and the engine room was alerted to standby for immediate action.

The engines were stopped at 4:00 a.m., then ordered ahead dead slow after a distinct green light from a small boat was seen right off the bow. *Carpathia*'s whistle sounded to let those in the boats know they had been seen.

At 4:10 a.m. Boat No. 2 was alongside and women were helped aboard through the gangway on the starboard side. Officer Boxhall and one crewman were the only men among the boats twenty-five occupants. The remainder were women.

Emotionally shaken and chilled to the bone, Officer Boxhall was taken to the bridge where he told Rostron the horror of what happened.

The first light of a pink dawn revealed a flotilla of tiny boats that dotted a sea choked with ice. Many would later relate how the ugly tragedy had unfolded into the beauty and spectacular color of the morning light reflected in the surrounding ice.

Soon after more of *Titanic*'s boats came alongside as the *Carpathia* steamed through the tiny fleet at dead slow.

One by one they came, their occupants carefully brought aboard under the watchful and compassionate eyes of *Carpathia*'s passengers who lined the rails, now fully aware of what had occurred.

Finally the overturned collapsible B was alongside with over twenty wearied survivors standing on the bottom of the over-turned boat leaning this way and that in a desperate balancing attempt to keep it from capsizing.

Among the occupants of this boat was Chief Baker Charles Joughin who had merrily stepped into the water as the *Titanic* sank beneath his feet. Having consumed a goodly amount of alcohol before the ship sank, he had been swimming about in the frigid water for two hours seemingly unconcerned and oblivious to the cold.

Shortly after 8:00 a.m., with sparkling character to the last, Officer Lightoller climbed the ladder to safety—the last *Titanic* survivor to come aboard.

Thirteen *Titanic* lifeboats were hoisted aboard and six were set adrift in the sea which was now becoming wind blown and choppy.

Bruce Ismay, who had boarded around 6:15 a.m., was in shock and privately under a doctor's care.

As the *Carpathia* combed the area searching for more survivors, a prayer service was arranged by Captain Rostron as the ship came over the co-ordinates where the *Titanic* had sunk.

After one last circle was made around the site, Rostron ordered the *Carpathia* to set a course west for New York. While there was great anguish and heartbroken tears among those survivors who felt their loved ones might still be adrift on the sea, they were also encouraged in believing other vessels might also have rescued survivors too.

The *Californian*, which had arrived on the scene as the last lifeboat was brought aboard, remained at the site searching for other survivors.

Because an enormous field of ice had blocked her progress, the *Carpathia* had to sail for several hours around the mass to eventually find clear water to resume her passage west.

In a solemn service held at 4:00 p.m., with engines stopped and the ship's flag at half-mast, *Carpathia*'s crewmen along with an Episcopal monk committed four of *Titanic*'s dead to the deep.

After recuperating somewhat, Ismay sent a wireless to the White Star office in New York with the official news that the *Titanic* had sunk with serious loss of life after hitting an iceberg. A second wireless requested the White Star liner *Cedric* be detained until the *Carpathia* arrived in order to facilitate immediate passage of *Titanic*'s crew back to England.

Hard as it must have been, and so soon after coming aboard, officer Lightoller and his crewmen had prepared a complete list of the survivors. The list was then given to wireless operator Cottam who by this time had been on duty for over twenty-four hours. It is here, one might imagine, that errors in the transmissions sent by the exhausted Cottam and received by those waiting for information, caused considerable agony. Incoming messages, including one from President Howard Taft requesting information on his aide Archibald Butt, were not acknowledged and simply ignored.

The first official word of *Titanic*'s desperate call for assistance reached the *New York Times* by way of a wireless bulletin at 1:20 a.m. Monday, April 15th, in time for the early morning edition. But due to vague information and poor wireless reception few hard facts were known. This resulted in the release of absurd and embellished errors. One banner head line would read, "All passengers saved, *Titanic* being towed to Halifax." Soon, however, after reports trickled in endorsed by Ismay himself, the true facts about the disaster and the shocking numbers that were lost were confirmed. The accurate figures of those lost would not be known until April 17th. Of the 2,224 passengers and crew aboard, 1,517 would be lost.

As a thunderstorm swept across the area, the *Carpathia* was warped in the Cunard Pier 54, at 9:30 p.m. on Thursday, April 18th, the exact point of her departure eight days before.

Thousands of people flocked to the wharf to catch a glimpse of the survivors who disembarked. News reporters in vain attempts to gain space on the pilot vessel that met the *Carpathia* were now swarming over the docks to get first hand accounts of the disaster. Still seemingly stunned, many of the survivors either did not hear or ignored the shouted questions hurled at them from the hungry correspondents.

Having lost everything in the sinking, many of the survivors were dressed in clothes given to them by *Carpathia*'s passengers. Worst off were those third-class passengers who, having lost all that they owned, were left to whatever relief assistance offered by the Red Cross and other charitable organizations.

Also there promptly to meet the *Carpathia* was Senator William Alden Smith of the Senate Committee on Commerce. After hastened conferences with President Taft and Attorney General Wickersham, who cleared the way for the subpoena of the British crewmen, Smith had been appointed to chair the sub-committee which would investigate the loss of the *Titanic*.

Smith found his way aboard the *Carpathia* to locate and confer with Bruce Ismay. Upon leaving the ship, Smith related to reporters that his committee would not be deterred by opposition from the White Star Line or British authorities.

Lacking experience with matters of the sea or knowledge of shipping the members of the committee included six Senators: George C. Perkins, California; Jonathan Bourne, Jr., Oregon; Theodore Burton, Ohio; Furnifold M. Simmons, North Carolina; Francis G. Newlands, Nevada; and Duncan U. Fletcher, Florida.

Nonetheless, through his quick action in preventing the fleeing of the British crew he was able to interrogate those associated with the disaster and its aftermath while details were still so fresh in their minds.

After all, serious questions, the answers to which could only be given by the crewmen and officers, had to be addressed. Was the obvious incompetence of the crew the cause for the loss of so many American lives? How could so many women and children be lost when so many of the ship's crew had been saved?

Twenty-nine of *Titanic*'s crew who had not been sub-poenaed were aboard the steamer Lapland ready to depart for England when they were served with subpoenas that prevented their departure. Another five who were able to depart on the *Lapland* were intercepted enroute by a federal marshal aboard a tug, who served and returned them for the inquiry.

In an obvious ploy to avoid further testimony, after three unsuccessful requests, Bruce Ismay tried to return to England or his offices in New York, but was detained.

Testifying in both New York and in Washington, eighty-two witnesses were interrogated during hearings that lasted seventeen days between April 19th and May 25th.

Senator Smith failed to secure the right for those in-volved in the disaster to sue the White Star Line for negli-gence. He did, however, succeed in bringing out into the open the related shortcomings and incompetence of the White Star Line which contributed wholly to the tragedy.

Additionally, he recommended three pieces of asso-ciated legislation. First, he submitted a resolution in con-junction with the House of Representatives to create an hon-orary medal to be presented by President Taft to Captain Arthur Rostron on behalf of the American people. Second, he intro-duced Senate Bill 6976 that would provide for a review and re-evaluation of statutes associated with marine legislation. Third, he submitted a joint legislative resolution to create a maritime commission to investigate the laws and regulations governing the building of and the equipment installed on all ocean-going vessels.

Queen's Road, Harland & Wolff shipyard men leaving work.

Starboard bow view of *Titanic* fully framed with *Olympic* fully plated alongside.

Port stern view of *Titanic*'s launch.

The completed *Titanic* in Belfast Lough with accompanying tugs.

First Class suite B-57

View #1. from author's collector print series,
Titanic....That Night.

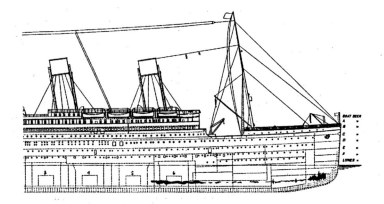

Naval architect Edward Wilding was head draftsman at Harland and Wolff at the time of the *Titanic* disaster. Based on eyewitness accounts and interrogation during the British Inquiry he testified that the iceberg penetrated the hull at least three feet at Hold #1 and in sufficient bulk to damage a wall adjacent to a winding stairway. No one knows the exact configuration of that hole as it was immediately masked by the explosion of incoming sea water. This gaping hole, however, was certainly large enough to have admitted a portion of the iceberg into the hull at least three feet.

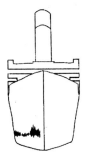

View #2. from author's collector print series,
Titanic....That Night.

View #3. from author's collector print series,
Titanic....That Night.

J. Clary ink drawing

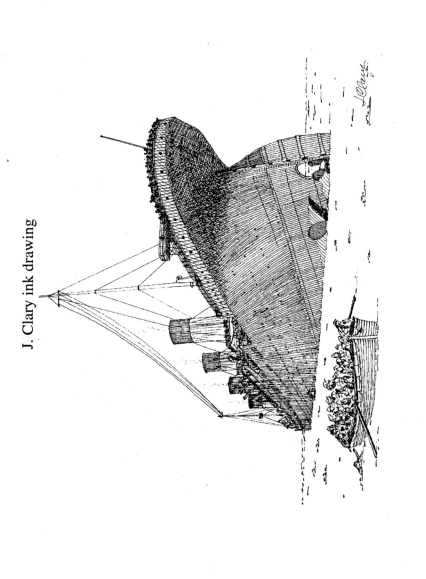

View #4. from author's collector print series,
Titanic....That Night.

Searchlight on the bridge of the White Star liner *Teutonic*, which sailed the Atlantic twenty years before the *Titanic*. (Mariners' Museum, Newport News, VA)

J. Clary ink drawing based on scenes
from the James Cameron movie *Titanic*.

Chapter Nine

Strange Theories

Voices of Titanic's past,
Tell us how her fate was cast.
Hear their voices, the story true,
Know the horror that they knew.

Whom are we to believe? There are countless con-
flicting accounts that cover almost every detail of the *Titanic*
disaster from surviving passengers and crew. Many of these
accounts were taken from stunned survivors by a multitude
of anxious reporters soon after the *Carpathia* arrived in New
York. The reporters were driven by the earth-shattering excitement over the loss of the great ship, which offered the
biggest news story of the time. Should we believe these newspaper accounts? Do we believe the accounts of tragedies in
the newspapers today?

To analyze and detail all of these true, sensational and
in some cases bizarre *Titanic* stories would surely fill numerous volumes. Covered here are only some of the more famous ones.

Was there a fire raging on the *Titanic* that was finally
extinguished when the vessel sank? According to the late J.
Dilley, a surviving fireman, that is exactly what happened.

Dilley and one hundred and fifty of his fellow crew
members had returned to England aboard the Red Star liner
Lapland. He related this story upon his arrival. His account
appeared in the 1912 memorial edition, *Story of the Wreck of
the Titanic, The Ocean's Greatest Disaster,* By D. H. Walter.
This volume was released shortly after the disaster and has
the distinction of leaning quite heavily toward fiction.

However, strong evidence points to the fact that there was a fire. On Saturday, April 13th, Captain Smith was reported to have been relieved to hear from his chief engineer Joseph Bell that a fire, which had been burning for nearly two weeks in Boiler Room No. 6, had finally been put out.

Fireman Dilley, who had also served as a fireman on the *Oceanic*, stated that from the day the vessel departed Southampton it was his daily duty, together with eleven other men to fight the fire. According to Dilley, at no time did they have the fire under control.

Even though the firemen were alarmed about the raging fire and were not allowed to mingle with passengers, they were still told to keep their mouths shut to avoid the spread of any panic.

Dilley stated that the fire started in bunker No. 6 where hundreds of tons of coal was stored. Coal on the top of this bunker was kept wet to prevent a fire. The coal being wet near the top of the bunker actually prevented the fire from spreading upward.   Near the bottom of the bunker the coal had dried out, and there the fire was raging.

Two stokers from every four-hour watch fought the fire. This meant that twelve men worked at the task every twenty-four hour period from the day they sailed until the vessel struck the iceberg.

There was talk among these men that upon arrival in New York, they would have to empty the bunkers and then rely on fireboats there to extinguish the fire. According to Dilley, not until the iceberg opened up the hull beneath the bunker was the fire put out.

The *Titanic*'s Chief Engineer Bell had his own version of the story. He too mentioned that the fire raged uncontrollably from sailing day until the afternoon of April 13th. However, he added that it was necessary to remove the coal from the forward sections two and three on the starboard side. This, according to him, weakened the bulkheads there because they did not have the supporting strength of the coal within. Weaker because the coal was not inside or adjacent to them, the bulkheads did not hold when the water came rushing in.

That is why when Bell received word that the forward bunker had given away he woefully declared, "My God, we are lost."

A corroborating and interesting piece of evidence that the coal was removed from those starboard bunkers comes from Second Class passenger Lawrence Beesley's account.

Beesley was very observant and overly curious about even the smallest details of his passage.

He had noticed and called attention to the fact that the *Titanic* had been listing (leaning) to port. He pointed this out to those sitting with him at the purser's table in the saloon on Sunday, April 14th. He noted that most of the time the horizon was visible through the portholes on the port side while only sky was visible on the starboard side.

The purser stated that this was probably because more coal had been used from the starboard side. This noticeable list was most likely caused by the removal of the coal from the starboard bunkers referred to by Chief Engineer Bell.

On an absolutely still night at sea sound can travel for miles. Strangely enough, the voices of fishermen trolling in their boats can be heard, not distinctly, but heard nonetheless for a great distance across the water.

Was there an explosion that accompanied the sinking of the *Titanic*?

The strange manner in which sound travels across the sea could have been the reason why descriptions vary about the big noise heard by many that night before the *Titanic* sank.

Several surviving crewmen testified to this noise in the Senate Inquiry. Steward George Frederick Crowe heard a kind of muffled explosion at a very great distance although

he was not very far away. Assistant Cook John Collins testified that the ship exploded in the water. Able Seaman John
Buley heard a little roar; Officer Herbert John Pitman heard
four reports like the reports from a big gun in the distance.
He assumed that it was the sound of the bulkheads going and
doubted that the sound came from the boilers exploding as
there was little steam in them - they had been drawn or cooled
by this time - for about two and one-half hours. He added
that the explosion came after the ship was entirely submerged;
Seaman Harold Lowe heard four explosions; and Seaman
George Thomas Rowe heard a sort of rumbling rather than an
explosion.

Some surviving passengers also reported hearing noise
ranging from "a sort of rumbling," heard by Major Arthur
Peuchen to "the last boiler explosion that tore the ship to
pieces," heard by Mrs. E. W. Carter.

What should be taken as the more reliable description
of the "noise" heard at that time comes from the survivors
whose accounts are considered to be the most accurate. Those
being the very descriptive accounts of Lawrence Beesley,
Archibald Gracie, and Second Officer Charles Lightoller,
found in *The Story of the Titanic as told by its Survivors.*

Lawrence Beesley described the noise as partly a rattle,
partly a groan, and partly a smash; not the sudden roar as an
explosion would be but rather prolonged like the roll and clash
of thunder. This, he believed, was caused by the ship's ma-
chinery tearing loose and falling as the aft end of the ship
rose high in the air.

Archibald Gracie's account of the noise is similar to
that of Lawrence Beesley.

Second Officer Lightoller described the sound as a
"hollow rumbling roar," thought to have been caused by the
boilers leaving their beds and tumbling down through the
bulkheads.

The contemporary versions of *Titanic*'s foundering covered in recent volumes and current films would lead one to believe that the great ship broke in two on the surface of the sea before it sank.

Having always endeavored to perpetuate the accuracy of history whenever and however I can, I am bothered by so called new information that ignores historical record without fully offering opposing views on the subject.

If such a new account, documentary, or film so captures and mesmerizes the attention of today's masses, will that information thereafter be taken as gospel? I am afraid that it will.

There are many *Titanic* survivors who claimed that the vessel broke in two on the surface. However, there is a great preponderance of evidence pointing to the fact that it did not.

At the top of the list of those who stated that this did not occur is Second Officer Charles Lightoller. During questioning in the Senate Inquiry, officer Lightoller was asked, "Did you leave the ship?"

Lightoller answered, "No, the ship left me."

Lightoller, in other words, remained on the ship rendering service to the very last.

This theory is not a new one as we might be led to believe by contemporary accounts. Lightoller related that at the time the *Titanic* was sinking beneath him, he was but a mere twelve feet from the area where the vessel was said to have separated.

The alleged "weak area" of the vessel was that area known as the "expansion joint," which extended transversely across the deck, but only through the Boat Deck and Decks A and B. It was built into the ship to ease the "flex" of the vessel in heavy seas.

According to Lightoller just a few seconds before the *Titanic* was thought to have broken in two, he stepped across this expansion joint and almost immediately thereafter the ship sank beneath him intact.

Another credible description was offered by Lawrence Beesley. Although Beesley also heard the noise associated with the vessel's aft end raising up, he stated that after the noise abated, the *Titanic*, "was still upright like a column."

In that upright position for an estimated five minutes, Beeseley added, "Then, first sinking back a little at the stern, I thought, she slid slowly forwards through the water and dived slantingly down."

Able Seaman Ernest Archer testified in the Senate Inquiry that while he was watching the ship (*Titanic*) all the time, there was nothing that gave him an impression that it had broken in two.

Major Arthur Peuchen stated in the inquiry that while he heard a low rumbling sound that he believed was a series of explosions, at that time the vessel was intact.

The late *Titanic* survivor Eva Hart empathically declared in a recent prime-time television special that the *Titanic* broke in two on the surface. However, later in that same special she claimed to have seen the vessel sink with all the lights still lit. Seven year-old Eva was traveling with her parents, Mr. and Mrs. Benjamin Hart.

The late Second Class passenger Edwina (Troutt) McKenzie related to me in a telephone interview that she could not take her eyes off the liner as it sank. Miss McKenzie was twenty-seven years old at the time the *Titanic* went down. Although she stated that there was a terrible noise, "She sank gracefully, she went down very, very gracefully." This is hardly the description one might expect to hear about a sinking vessel that supposedly broke in two. The full text of McKenzie's interview appears later in this chapter.

It is old theory that those who claimed the vessel separated were misled by the number one stack falling into the sea in an immense shower of sparks. It may be an old theory but it is one that at least offers a sound explanation of what could have been mistakenly seen as the breakup.

Imagine the thunderous clamor, the shriek of tearing metal, and the likely spectacular display of showering sparks that must have occurred when this stack crashed into the sea. The fall of this seventy-two foot, oval-shaped object, measuring nineteen feet at its most narrow width, surely could have offered those in lifeboats, a great distance away, the idea that the ship was breaking in two.

How does one account for the wreck resting in two main pieces on the ocean floor nearly 2,000 feet apart? Here is proof the vessel definitely broke in two, but it most likely did so during her 13,000 foot plunge, after she had left the surface.

Long ago the US Navy performed a study in an effort to determine what course a sinking vessel might take on the way down and how it might land on the bottom. Vessels were intentionally scuttled bow first, stern first and from both the port and starboard sides. Due to a number of factors such as the configuration of the vessel, its tonnage, and its cargo, there was no set pattern as to the manoeuvres they went through on the way down or in what position they landed.

It was determined that when a vessel sinks it is like flipping a coin in the water. The vessel might circle, plane, or dive like a stone on the way down.

Just because the *Titanic*'s pieces are separated on the bottom does not necessarily mean that it broke at the surface.

I tend to believe the accounts of Officer Lightoller the top ranking surviving officer and Second Class passenger Lawrence Beesley. Their accounts are praised as being the most credible and accurate, yet they are all but neglected or forgotten in current versions. Who could best chronicle those critical moments other than Lawrence Beesley who offered such explicit detail and Officer Lightoller who was so close to the area of the alleged break.

Did inferior metal used in *Titanic*'s hull plating contribute to the sinking?

This theory contends that engineering impact studies performed on a soup plate size piece of metal retrieved from the wreck site of the *Titanic*, revealed that the metal was brittle. The study claimed that rather than bending under stress the metal easily shattered.

It was theorized that if the iceberg struck many of these inferior plates, it might have caused them all to disintegrate.

There is substantial proof that de-bunks this theory. The steel plating used on the *Olympic* and *Titanic* was the same Siemens-Martin formula steel used in the *Teutonic* and *Majestic*. These armed merchant cruisers were built in 1889 and 1890. This steel had good elastic properties, was resistant to corrosion, and was considered perfect for both manual and hydraulic riveting.

After twenty years of service, the hull plating of the *Teutonic* and *Majestic* were shown to be in excellent condition.

Further, after the *Olympic* collided with the HMS *Hawke* on September 20, 1911, although *Titanic*'s sister received extensive damage to her port bow plating, there was no evidence of the metal being shattered.

Moreover, the *Olympic*, built before, and with the same hull plating as *Titanic* had a thirty-year career.

As one might expect, many questions arose since the disaster, as to why this or that endeavor was not undertaken in order to save many more of *Titanic*'s victims. Some of these ideas seem quite plausible, some quite ludicrous.

Many students of the disaster question why when the ridiculous shortage of lifeboats was finally realized, did those left aboard not make rafts out of deck chairs or anything floatable at hand?

The *Titanic* certainly must have had a vast repair shop with generous lengths of wire, cable, or rope, along with the necessary tools to fashion make-shift rafts. One only need view the many interior photographs of the first, second, and third class areas to note the wooden doors, head and foot boards of beds, dining chairs, tables, benches, railings, and pillars, suitable for flotation. In cargo, there even was an un-determined quantity of "old oak beams."

The sea was absolutely calm, and had not confusion and over-confidence, rather than ingenuity reigned, hurriedly fashioned jury-rigged rafts could easily have supported and sustained many more of those who were needlessly lost.

It is bewildering why the will to survive did not over-take, guide, and drive those helpless souls into action to save themselves. Perhaps by the time the last die-hard believers were convinced that the *Titanic* was definitely going to sink, it was far too late for this kind of action.

When dawn broke the morning of the sinking it was said that those in lifeboats were completely surrounded by a vast field of ice floe and icebergs, a spectacular sight in the early sunrise.

I have been asked many times why couldn't passen-gers have been taken off the *Titanic* and transferred by the lifeboats to one of these large icebergs to await rescue? This is a foolish and highly dangerous notion at best. For those unaware of the threat icebergs pose, the question deserves an answer.

There have been many instances where foolhardy mariners tried to either moor their vessel to, or actually board an iceberg and met with near catastrophe.

An iceberg's mass and beauty almost makes them seem docile and harmless. But, as often happens, if a large enough piece of a berg breaks off, in seconds the entire mass can suddenly turn over, causing a rush of massive waves by its sudden change of configuration. Even large vessels lying a good distance away could be upset or destroyed.

The precarious instability of icebergs is best illustrated with an incident that occurred when two sailors were trying to attach an anchor to a berg. They had scarcely begun to hack away at the ice when suddenly the entire mass split in two from top to bottom, the two halves plunging into the sea with a thunderous crash. Luckily the men escaped with their lives.

Another foolhardy incident took place near Temple Bay, Labrador, when two young officers from a French man-of-war, ignoring all warnings, boarded a nearby iceberg for a picnic. The warm calm morning evaporated any fear of danger, and by noon the two had scaled the glistening palace walls to reach the very top of the berg. There they shouted and drank toasts to their fellow officers. They hacked at the ice and made fun of the dread supposedly attached to the beautiful wonder of the sea. Finally finished with their horseplay, the men clambered back down to their ship. No sooner had they boarded when the giant iceberg broke up like an eggshell into infinite fragments which filled and roiled the surrounding sea.

Another question often posed by many armchair *Titanic* enthusiasts asks: Would the *Titanic* have survived had it struck the iceberg head on, instead of striking it on the starboard bow and side?

Of course one's first quick reaction to avoid hitting an object coming straight at you is to swerve away from that object. So too on the *Titanic* that fateful night. When the lookout telephoned the bridge with the alarming, "Iceberg right ahead!" it is doubtful that there was even a split-second hesitation to ponder whether or not to hit the berg head on.

In November 1879, the Guion liner *Arizona* struck an

iceberg head-on and did more than survive.

Bound for Liverpool from New York, the *Arizona* encountered a thick Newfoundland Grand Banks fog. In the dense murk, the *Arizona* crashed into an iceberg at fifteen knots smashing in twenty-five feet of her bow. Some passengers, knocked off their feet, scurried on deck to see the bow of their ship buried deep into a giant berg that towered sixty feet above the ship.

Remarkably, the *Arizona* withstood the crash and limped safely into St. Johns, Newfoundland, where it was quickly repaired. A wooden bow was fitted to the ship, which enabled her to race back to Liverpool in six days, seventeen hours, and thirteen minutes!

While the *Arizona*'s master, Captain Jones, was held accountable for the tragedy and lost his Master's Certificate, the *Arizona*'s fame blossomed. Ocean travelers were convinced that the incident offered absolute proof of the strength of the *Arizona*. They believed that if the vessel was strong enough to crash into an iceberg head-on and survive, it was indeed a safe ship. As a result, more passengers booked passage on the *Arizona* than on any other ocean liner of the time.

Additional proof that a vessel can survive a head-on collision can be drawn from the *Andrea Doria - Stockholm* disaster which occurred in July of 1956.

The 524-foot Swedish liner *Stockholm* struck the starboard side of the *Andrea Doria* head on. Seventy-five feet of the Stockholm's bow was smashed in flat. Soon after the collision the *Stockholm* heeled dangerously down at the bow over four feet. Although her number 2 and 3 holds were sealed off and tight, there was already thirteen feet of water in the number 1 hold.

Quick action saved the vessel. Ninety-five tons of fresh water from the ship's forward tanks was pumped overboard, and twenty-five tons of fuel was transferred from the starboard to the port tanks in order to right the vessel.

Not knowing the underwater configuration of the iceberg, nor what damage that unknown configuration, spur, or mass could have inflicted on the hull, it is anyone's guess. However, if less than five of *Titanic*'s watertight compartments would not have been holed from a bow-on collision, more than likely she could have survived at least for a greater length of time.

One 1912 newspaper article ironically claimed that although the *Titanic*'s lavish grand dining room was furnished at the cost of $15,000, she did not have binoculars for lookouts in the crow's nest.

Lookout Frederick Fleet, who was in the crow's nest when the *Titanic* struck the iceberg, testified in the Senate Inquiry that although he had asked for glasses prior to sailing, none were made available to him.

Lookout Archie Jewell who was in the crow's nest just before Fleet's watch, testified in the inquiry that he had used glasses on the *Oceanic* for seven or eight voyages before sailing on the *Titanic*. He also added that he considered the glasses to be very useful and that although there was a box in the crow's nest for the glasses, no glasses were in the box.

Whether binoculars would have been of any use that dark night is questionable. On that moonless night there was not even the slightest ripple on the sea. There was not the least bit of sea action to lap against the bottom of the iceberg to thereby catch the faint reflection of starlight. The sea was so calm that stars low on the horizon could be seen reflected in the sea.

With a pair of powerful binoculars I have looked at the stars at sea and followed their configurations down to the horizon. Although the sea was pitch black, there was a definite horizon line visible which separated the stars from the sea.

If the lookouts, in a known iceberg danger area, had carefully scrutinized the horizon line with binoculars, they might have easily spotted the iceberg as it blocked out the star patterns. What could have hampered the lookout's view, however, was a slight haze that the *Titanic* was sailing into at the time. The iceberg was sighted when it emerged from this haze.

It was said that the lookouts were expected to remain alert and rely on good eyesight. However, once you attain good night vision, your eyesight it would seem, could only be more enhanced with binoculars, even on a dark night. There remains a nagging question. How could the use of binoculars have reduced good eyesight?

Frederick Fleet was considered an outcast by many surviving *Titanic* officers because in the inquiry, he revealed the lack of binoculars in the crow's nest. He sailed for twenty-four years after the sinking of the *Titanic* and then worked at Harland and Wolff until his retirement. After that he peddled newspapers on the streets of Southampton. Said to have been despondent over his wife's death, he took his own life by hanging on January 10, 1965, at the age of seventy-six.

Far more important than the absence of binoculars was the lack of a searchlight. While the *Titanic* had a powerful Morse lamp that could be seen for miles, it was not fitted with this essential piece of gear. If she would have had a searchlight and used it, this disaster more than likely would not have happened.

Living in St. Clair, Michigan, along the St. Clair River where large chunks of ice drift down from upper Lake Huron in winter, I have often seen big lake freighters and ocean going vessels use their searchlights to illuminate hazardous objects far ahead of their position. Useless in fog, heavy rain, or snow squalls, these lights can throw a bright beam for miles on a clear night.

The earliest operational searchlight, known as Mr.

Wilde's electric light, was carried on the H.M.S. *Comet* in 1874. It had 11,000 candlepower and had a range of one mile. In 1880, a searchlight known as Gramme's light used on the H.M.S. *Northampton* had a 20,000 candlepower.

The Francis Searchlight Company of Bromley Cross, Bolton, United Kingdom have manufactured searchlights since 1901. According to Mr. Tom Needham, an official at this company, searchlights were fitted to warships and those vessels navigating the Suez Canal around the late 1800's. Their use was restricted to warships, custom boats, dredgers, and of all ships - ice breakers!

Mr. Needham also pointed out that searchlights used in that era were of the carbon arc principle, which therefore made those units very heavy and cumbersome, requiring special training for their use.

In order to attract subsidies, the White Star liner *Teutonic*, launched on January 19, 1889, was supposed to have doubled as an armed merchant cruiser during wartime. By August of that year, however, she was in service, bound for New York, as one of White Star's majestic liners.

She had the distinction of holding the Blue Ribband too, but for only two months in 1891. She is mentioned here because she did carry a searchlight, which in effect was fitted for her supposed wartime role.

So here is a White Star liner equipped with a searchlight, and in service as an ocean liner on the north Atlantic more than twenty years before the *Titanic*.

Searchlights were important enough to have been used on ice breakers, and on White Star's *Teutonic* twenty years before *Titanic*. It appears that this was a negligent shortcoming because it was not part of the standard gear on the *Titanic*.

Could the *Titanic* have remained afloat longer had she kept her engines in reverse? Here is another question often asked.

First of all, *Titanic*'s officers were unsure of the damage sustained to the hull for some time. By the time the vessel was sounded to determine that she would in fact founder, it was far too late for this manoeuvre if it was even considered.

Given that the vessel was taking an estimated twelve tons of water per minute while underway, it is reasonable to presume that had she continued to back, then much of that water might have been sucked out of her. Or at least through her reversing motion the flow of water might have been neutralized to the point that a minimum amount of sea came in.

One can easily verify the plausibility of this theory by moving a partially filled holed container, similar in shape to the *Titanic*'s hull, in a tank of water away from the hole. You will find that the incoming flow of water is not only somewhat neutralized but that some water actually comes out of the hole as well.

The theory also raises other questions. Would it have been necessary then to have kept *Titanic*'s engines in reverse all the way to her destination? Would the maneuver have bought precious time? Perhaps so, but at some time, the lifeboats would have had to be lowered to facilitate a rescue, which could not be accomplished while underway.

Chapter Ten

Survivors' Tales

They were there - do you not believe?
They did not really mean to deceive.
They were stunned. They were in shock.
And the newsmen met them at the dock.

This interview with Edwina (Troutt) McKenzie, the oldest survivor of the *Titanic* disaster at the time, was taken June 18, 1981. Mrs. McKenzie appears on the survivor list as Miss E. Celia Troutt. She died in 1984, five months after celebrating her 100th birthday.

Having interviewed many other survivors during my research of the *Titanic*, I found that all of them were very young at the time (eight to ten years old) and were kept hidden or protected from witnessing much of the horrible event. Regretfully, I did not attempt to get these interviews sooner and feel saddened, because I had not gained some of the knowledge that I feel will be lost forever. During my life-long study of the disaster, I had many questions that seemingly others never thought to ask. Even from some of the best and supposedly accurate accounts, these questions went unanswered.

After searching out another very old survivor who had lived in Michigan (she had died just a few months before my attempts to reach her), I was interviewed on CBC radio. The interviewer talked with me privately and we traded some survivors' names. I was surprised to learn that Mrs. McKenzie was still alive and living in California, for I had information otherwise. I immediately contacted her and thus came the following interview.

Truly *the* voice of the past on the *Titanic* disaster, Mrs. McKenzie was a single, twenty-seven-year-old traveling in second class. From her vivid account of the event came positive answers to questions about the rigid class structure, the fire aboard the *Titanic*, the songs being played, the lifeboats, the iceberg, and many other facts that were only hearsay before. What was uppermost important was the fact that Mrs. McKenzie actually saw the *Titanic* sink and could relate her story as an adult at the time.

CLARY: Mrs. McKenzie, how old were you when you were on the *Titanic*?

McKENZIE: At the present time I am ninety-six and on July the eighth I'll be ninety-seven. Ha-ha, I'm growing old.

CLARY: Now, that means that you would have been about twenty-seven at the time?

McKENZIE: Yes, you're correct, you're a good mathematician.

CLARY: Were you coming to America for the first time?

McKENZIE: No, that was my second visit. I had a married sister that lived in the United States, and I came over and stayed with her a while and she lived in the East and I couldn't stand the climate, so I went back home. Then I got back home and she became a mother, and my mother. . .oh, she was so anxious to have me come out to see the new baby, and so forth, you know. So I had to please my mother and that's why I happened to come back again.

CLARY: Now, leading up to the boarding of the *Titanic,* or at least when you knew you were going to be traveling on the *Titanic*, did anything happen that [interrupted]

McKENZIE: Uh, there were uh. . .I was supposed to be on another boat and this boat was at its moorings, the *New York* I believe it was. . .and the suction of the *Titanic* when she started was so great it drew those boats from their moorings. So we stopped the *Titanic*, and got the boats back, and then uh. . .we went out slowly and everything was OK.

CLARY: When that happened did that kind of make you worry a bit?

McKENZIE: [Didn't hear last question] We got over to France and we took on different people there and when we left France we went to Ireland. And uh. . .I don't know if this is too long for you. . .as we took the passengers on in Ireland, joining me in my stateroom was a girl by the name of Nora Keane and she said to me, "Glory be to God, you know, I should never be on this boat, it'll never reach New York." And she had a most unpleasant journey because all she could think of was she shouldn't have been on the boat, because it'll never reach New York.

CLARY: She was just afraid of it then?

McKENZIE: Uh-huh. So we went to church on Sunday, and uh. . .the weather was so bitterly cold and the wind was blowing, and uh. . .after church we went to dinner and a Mr. Milling (Jacob C. Milling) at my table said to me, "You know, we are now in midocean." He said, "I bought a ticket and my wife or anyone else didn't know I was on this boat." He said, "Now I'm able to send a cable to her, and we are in midocean!" Well, that was Sunday noon, and people will say that we were going too fast; well, Sunday, if you recall, was four days out, and we were only half the journey there, so I'm defending the White Star Line. Why do people say she was going too fast?

CLARY: Oh, I see. Well, now, this Nora Keane, did her experience make you wonder a little bit about the *Titanic?* Weren't you kind of afraid to go on it too?

McKENZIE: Well, she kept on and on, so, uh. . .Sunday night was unusually cold and I let her go to bed and I thought she'd be to sleep, but when I got to the stateroom she wasn't. She said, "Is that you?" I said yes. . .Oh, and she went on and on about the boat and not reaching New York. And I said, "Please don't talk about that anymore, I don't want to hear it." And then I thought oh, if anything happens, could happen in the night, I'm not going to undress, so I, haha, didn't undress, I wanted to be clothed in my. . .of course, I had my nightgown over some of my clothes, I didn't entirely undress.

CLARY: Were you traveling with your husband?

McKENZIE: No, I was with. . .my name was Troutt, you know, I was a single girl. It's taken from the German name of Traut, but that's our name anyhow.

CLARY: Do you recall or did you hear about a lady passenger who, upon boarding the *Titanic,* saw the face of a stoker atop one of the smokestacks?

McKENZIE: I didn't hear that before, haven't heard that.

CLARY: What class were you traveling in?

McKENZIE: Second class, my stateroom was 202, I think. E, Deck E.

CLARY: Can you estimate how long it was after the *Titanic* struck the iceberg that you were told to get into a lifeboat?

McKENZIE: Oh, that I wouldn't know. I don't know when she struck because I was asleep. I don't know how long that was. . .but uh. . .when I awoke, you know, I jumped out of bed and went out to see what was wrong, and uh. . .I met a young fella and I said something's wrong with the ship. "Oh, no," he said, "It's just stopped," said, "Just uh. . .it isn't anything." Oh, I said, you don't stop in mid-ocean, we're not taking on passengers or baggage or anything. Something has happened to the ship. And he said, "No." So I went up on deck. I went up to the, oh, I don't know, I went up and up and up, and I met this young boy, and both of us went up and the captain came after us and said, "What are you doing up here?" I said, I came to see what's wrong with the ship. He said,

"You better get back to bed." He said, "It's too cold for you." So I got back and I met the purser and I said that something's wrong with the ship. He said, "We've just stopped for awhile but we're moving on again." And he said, "You better get back into bed or else you'll catch your death of cold." But uh. . .that's the warning that we got, they just told us that everything was OK. Then finally, as I left him, there was some man saying, or the purser was saying, "All passengers put on their life preservers and get up on the boat deck." And this man said to me, "He's making fun of you." And I really thought he was.

Well, we got up on the boat deck, and I was surprised to see so many boats had gone, and then this fella came to me and said, "Oh, my," he said, "You are the ladies opposite the stateroom of the two Spanish ladies; I wonder if they heard the order. And he said, "Will you come with me?" So we went down, and those ladies were sleeping and he awakened them and they dressed, and both of them were saved. And the boy was drowned [the crew member who woke the ladies] but the two ladies were saved. And I never knew their names because they didn't speak English.

CLARY: Were you afraid at the time?

McKENZIE: Well, uh, no, I thought with God all things are possible, this is my. . .the ending. You know, we all have to die sometime or other and I thought this was my death, I'm going to have a watery grave. . .ha. . .and I was Scot enough to think it won't cost anything. . .to be buried.

CLARY: Do you remember when you came on deck where the boats were loading, was it difficult to hear or speak because of the roar of steam?

McKENZIE: Well, uh. . .it all depends on what part of the boat you were at, you know. At that time where I was it was quiet but some people naturally must have heard the steam.

CLARY: It was reported to have been very loud, like

a hundred locomotives releasing steam.

McKENZIE: You know, two people cannot tell you the same story that were on that boat if they were in different parts. That boat was so huge what happened in front you don't know what happened at the back. So you cannot get two stories alike. Isn't that so?

CLARY: If there was one single thing that stayed in your mind the most about the whole *Titanic* incident all these years. . .maybe it was something humorous. . .something strange. . .what would that be?

McKENZIE: Well, you know, I saved the baby of a little mother, and the little mother was from Peru, and uh. . .she was a third-class passenger and she was separated from her baby. And uh. . .the baby was brought up on the starboard side of the deck by a man, and she was on the port side. The poor soul was separated, you see? So this man was there, and he had the baby in his arms and he was told to STAND BACK...STAND BACK, THE ENGLISH. [Apparently, the man with the baby was a steerage passenger and was being stopped from getting into or near a lifeboat.]

Well, he said, "I don't want to be saved but save the baby." So I said, "Well, I'll save it." So I saved the baby, and I never knew until sixty years after the name of the child or anything about its passage. It appears that the mother was just a seventeen-year-old married woman whose husband lived in Pennsylvania and she was from Peru and was bringing the baby home to her husband. [It was not until Edwina McKenzie appeared on the Phil Donahue show during a telephone conversation with that baby's sister that she found out—sixty years later—what the name of that child, who had since died, was.]

CLARY: Do you know the number of the lifeboat you were in?

McKENZIE: Thirteen.

CLARY: When lifeboat No. 13 was being lowered,

it was supposed to have been lowered directly in the path of a big spout of water from the condenser exhaust coming out the side of the ship Do you recall any difficulties when they lowered your lifeboat?

McKENZIE: Yes. In the path, sure. We never thought our boat would touch the water; we had a terrible time with it. The davits were frozen, and uh. . .we had an awful time, and then nobody had any knives with them to cut the ropes or something. . .I forget.

CLARY: How many were in your boat? [Sixty-four, according to the Archibald Gracie account]

McKENZIE: Oh, that I wouldn't know, I don't remember. We could've taken more, but I don't, I truly don't, remember.

CLARY: When your boat was pulling away, was there fear of being pulled down by the suction?

McKENZIE: Yes.

CLARY: Did you actually watch the ship sink out of sight?

McKENZIE: I could not take my eyes off of her [answered without hesitation]; she just sank. . .I've always said gracefully, she went down very, very gracefully, and a terrible noise when she did. The engineers were all on duty, every one of them, and they all drowned.

CLARY: They say it's a very sad or eerie feeling when you see a ship sink. What was your feeling? Do you remember that?

McKENZIE: You bet. The feeling was very, very awful. Your heart goes down in your stomach, and your stomach isn't there anymore. Oh, my, it's a very terrible feeling. There isn't another feeling like it. And then, what made it so horrid was the screams of the people when they touched the water, you know. Fifteen hundred people were drowned at one time. When you hear fifteen hundred people screaming. . .I call it the scream of death. That's worse than any siren. .

.yes.

CLARY: Could you estimate how long after the sinking you could hear those screams?

McKENZIE: We heard them for an hour or more. . .Oh, dear.

CLARY: Do you remember who was in charge of your lifeboat? [Chief Stoker, Fireman Frederick Barrett]

McKENZIE: Oh, uh. . .I've forgotten his name now. I've forgotten but I went and saw him.

CLARY: Do you keep in touch with other survivors at all?

McKENZIE: No, I. . .they're so scattered. I uh. . .no. . .once in a while we get together, but they, uh. . .the lady from Santa Monica and one from Beverly Hills, but you can't get them to talk about it, they all. . .nobody likes to talk about it that was on it, only me, so I say I'm brazen. Ha-ha-ha. Don't you think?

CLARY: I think you're very grand about it. Now, do you remember the rockets going off?

McKENZIE: Oh, yes. Surely. You know, the rockets were terrible because they made us more afraid than we were already. Oh, yes.

CLARY: They made you more afraid? [Didn't hear question]

McKENZIE: Oh, they said. . .I heard the captain say to the crew, "This is it, everybody for themselves."

CLARY: You heard the captain say that?

McKENZIE: Yes, I heard the captain say that. I was in lifeboat thirteen, one of the last boats to leave. It couldn't have been the very last but one of the last to leave. The davits were frozen. We thought we'd never touch water but we did. [No. 13 lifeboat was reportedly lowered at 1:35 a.m.].

CLARY: How were you dressed? Did you have evening clothes on?

McKENZIE: Oh, no. I was in bed, so I was in my

nightgown, but I put on a big heavy coat. And uh. . .I went back to my stateroom and thought, well, would I save anything? Then I thought what's the use of saving anything, I know I'm gonna drown. And uh. . .I was reconciled to death. . .and so I could have saved many things, but I thought that this is it.

CLARY: Now, there is one question that I've asked other survivors, and of course they were very young at the time, but right after the *Titanic* hit the iceberg, it is recorded that it started up again. Do you remember that?

McKENZIE: Well, it has been so long ago, I don't really remember that. . .no I don't. [From what she related earlier, she would have been in bed at that time.] I know that the people were excited and they couldn't put on their life preservers. Oh, you'd be. . .you know. . .there wasn't any screaming or yelling. . .people were quiet but they were. . .then I looked up on the deck [from her lifeboat] and there was a priest or a man of the holy orders of some kind giving or saying prayers to them. They were all kneeling around. . .and people knew that the boat couldn't save them. And I think that was the most wonderful thing to see all those people kneeling down knowing that the boat was going down. Oh, the people were very orderly over such an ordeal. God gave them strength to. . .take what was coming to them. Isn't that something?

CLARY: It sure was. It's not like some of the early accounts that stated that there was a great deal of panic.

McKENZIE: No. There was bound to be some panic. . .yes. . .and in our boat there was the two little babies from France. The father was bringing them to the United States unbeknown to the mother. Both of the boys were in our lifeboat and they had a governess with them, and uh. . .they were saved. They couldn't speak English, they could only speak French, and there was a Mrs. Hayes from New York. She took them to her home, and there was an article in the paper with their pictures and their mother read of it in France, and the White Star Line let her come over and take her children home to France. One of them is still alive, but the other one died in the war.

CLARY: Were there any bad omens that you remember about the events that transpired?

McKENZIE: Ah, well, this woman that was in my stateroom kept saying I shouldn't have been on this boat, it will never reach New York, but other than that I didn't hear anything.

CLARY: I wonder why she came up with that idea.

McKENZIE: I don't know. She. . .uh. . .was an Irish woman returning to the United States and she had been home for a trip and I think was on the way back. She just kept on and on about this boat never reaching New York. Ha-ha, isn't that funny? You know, if I felt so strong in my mind that the boat would never reach New York, I wouldn't have gone on it. I don't know why she went on the boat when she felt it would never reach New York. She could have gotten off at France or Ireland.

CLARY: Was she saved?

McKENZIE: Oh, yes. She was saved and she lived in Pennsylvania, but she didn't live many years after. She was a very heavy lady, not very old. . .in her late forties, I guess. Oh, dear.

CLARY: Do you remember anything about the fire that was supposed to have been raging on the *Titanic*?

McKENZIE: Nearly all those ships were on fire, so of course there was some fire. Nearly all of them years ago used to be on fire. They couldn't help it. Men were fighting fires from the time they left Southampton. People don't know it but they usually are always on fire. I knew this from the fireman; [Fireman Barrett in her lifeboat] he told me so. Yes, they usually are. They have a hard time, those men. They drove a stoker up from below to man our boat, you know. I thought that was awful, and the poor fellow. . .he didn't have a life preserver on him, so I took the preserver off of the baby and gave it to him because I could keep the baby warm with my preserver and my big coat.

CLARY: When you were in the lifeboat, did you pick up anyone out of the water that was in your area?

McKENZIE: No, we did not and we didn't lose anybody either. There's plenty of stories about that, but we didn't. . .uh. . .our men. . .there were lights and our men were told to row to those lights. . .empty their. . .[passengers]. They thought there was a ship. . .empty your boats and come back and pick up more passengers. Well, our men rowed and rowed but that light was no nearer or no further or no nearer, and it was just as distinct as could be, but we never never could reach that light. They called it a mysterious light. Our men rowed and rowed and rowed and we were never. . .it seemed we never could get to that light.

CLARY: What time were you picked up in the morning?

McKENZIE: Oh, uh. . .that I don't know. To me it felt like seven o'clock, but we were picked up long before then. We saw the sun rise that morning, and uh. . .the uh. . .we saw the icebergs. We were in a field, a sea of ice, and they were iridescent, if you know what that is, and uh. . .the sunrise was most beautiful that morning, and all those, uh, icicles, they looked wonderful. I mean those icebergs that sunk the boat.

CLARY: Now, when you first got into your lifeboat and were rowing away, was there ice in the water then?

McKENZIE: Oh, surely. Yes. There was a sea of ice.

CLARY: Let's go back now aboard the *Titanic* again. There were reports about ice on the decks from the iceberg. Do you remember that?

McKENZIE: When the boat struck, I, uh, told Miss

Keane I'll go and see what's the matter, and I went and met a young boy from my table, and we went up and up and we got way up into the top of the ship and it was covered with pieces of ice. And uh, I was very blonde at the time and had long hair and a couple of braids, and one of the men said to me, "Hello, blondie, what's wrong with you?" Well, I said, "There's nothing wrong with me, I want to know what's wrong with the ship." So he said, "It isn't anything, we just grazed an iceberg." He gave me a little bit of ice, you know, and so uh. . .I. . .I had never seen an iceberg or even thought of one at the time. So I went down to my stateroom and told Miss Keane that it's all right. "Miss Keane," I said, "we just grazed an iceberg."

And she said, "My God, girl! Oh! Don't you know what an iceberg is?" And she raved and raved and knew for sure the boat would never reach New York. But I was very ignorant of icebergs. . .never heard of them or saw or thought of them before.

CLARY: About the old story that the band was play-ing "Nearer My God to Thee" as the *Titanic* was sinking. Were you in the area where the band was playing?

McKENZIE: Oh, yes. . .yes, sure I was, but the band. . .When I left the *Titanic*, the band wasn't playing "Nearer My God to Thee," or anything like that, they were playing waltz tunes, and I know that waltz tune, and I don't know why but I can remember it, but I think it must have been the tune that they always played at meals, and it goes like this [hums a few bars of the song]. . .and it goes on. . .a waltz tune. . .very nice it was. . .and all those men were drowned. . .terrible, isn't it? But I think it's terrible the loss of life. I. . .I can't understand why they let so many people drown. . .I don't. We had room for more people in our lifeboat, and I know that other lifeboats did too.

CLARY: Well, Mrs. Mckenzie, I want to thank you so much for your help.

McKENZIE: All right. Well, I wish you a happy day and, uh, keep smiling and keep happy.

It seems so grossly appalling that while so many *Titanic* passengers were lost there were at least two pet dogs saved.

Referred to as "the dog hero," a black Newfoundland named *Rigel*, said to have belonged to First Officer Murdoch, was to have swum in the icy sea for three hours after the *Titanic* sank. Jonas Briggs, a seaman aboard the *Carpathia* related the strange story of heroism.

It was claimed that the dog swam ahead of the fourth lifeboat picked up by the *Carpathia* and that its barking alerted those on the rescue ship of the lifeboat's position. It was believed that the cold and exhausted occupants of the boat, too weak to hail their location, might not have been seen were it not for the barking hero.

Rigel seemed oblivious to the cold and his long arduous swim in the frigid waters.

To show off some of the dogs owned by the first-class passengers, there was to be a dog show on the *Titanic*, which was scheduled for Monday, April 15th. Candidates for the show included passenger Harry Anderson's Chow, and Robert W. Daniel's champion French bulldog, *Gamon de Pycombe,* valued at $750. Then there was a Pomeranian owned by Margaret Hays of New York, Henry Harper's Pekinese, *Sun Yat Sen*, John Jacob Astor's Airedale, *Kitty*, and Helen Bishop's little *Frou Frou*, who, instead of being housed in *Titanic*'s new kennels, slept in her owner's bed.

If Captain Smith's Airedale and Officer Murdoch's *Rigel*, were aboard, and it hasn't been verified that they were, these prominent pets would most likely have joined in the show too.

Daily dog walking duty on *Titanic*'s spacious fantail was left up to various members of the crew.

After helping his young five-months pregnant wife into lifeboat No. 4, John Jacob Astor was denied the opportunity to join her. One could hardly blame him for trying because the boat, with no male passengers, only carried a total of forty occupants including crewmen.

Without making a fuss, Mr. Astor calmly assured his wife that with rescue vessels on the way, he would certainly be along to join her shortly. He then helped other ladies get into the boat.

Smiling and remaining calm, Astor waved good-bye as No. 4 was lowered away out of sight at 1:55 a.m. It was then time for him to perform one last act of mercy for a close friend. He descended to the dog kennels on F deck, where by now the cold sea was likely to be heard roaring in. Here he turned loose his Airedale and the other dogs that would have been trapped in their cages.

It was later related by his wife Madeleine, that as she tried to catch one final glimpse of her husband on the decks of the fast sinking ship, she caught sight of their dog *Kitty* running here and there on the slanting deck. One can only imagine what pangs of sorrow she must have felt, upon learning that neither her husband nor their Airedale survived.

In the BBC United Kingdom News Online story, *Nephew Angered by Tarnishing of Titanic Hero*, published Saturday, January 24, 1998, the nephew of First Officer William Murdoch criticized the blockbuster movie *Titanic* for tarnishing his reputation.

Officer Murdoch is portrayed committing suicide in the film but is considered a hero in his home town of Dalbeattie, Scotland. His nephew Scott, who takes objection to the suicide portrayal states, "From my own family connections and also from my father having spoke to various officers who survived, he didn't commit suicide."

It was known that those *Titanic* officers who commanded the lowering of the lifeboats were armed with pistols. Were they expecting chaos because they knew of the pitiful shortage of lifeboats or because of an expected stampede of men rather than women and children first?

If there was any panic aboard the *Titanic* it likely occurred during the lowering of boat No. 14 on the port side and Collapsible C and lifeboat No 1, the last two boats lowered on the starboard side.

As boat No. 14 was being loaded under the command of Officer Lowe, steerage passengers made an attempt to leap into the boat but were stopped when Lowe fired shots from his revolver along the side of the ship. This boat was lowered at 1:30 a.m.

And then, as they were assisting the lowering of Collapsible D on the port side at 2:05 a.m, passengers Hugh Woolner and Bjornstrom Steffanson heard a ruckus on the starboard side.

As they approached the commotion they observed Officer Murdoch firing his pistol into the air to ward off some men who made a rush into the boat. Woolner and Bjornstrom then helped pull the men out of the boat - some of them by their legs - so that some nearby steerage women could board the boat. It was here that the head of the White Star line, Bruce Ismay found his way into Collapsible C. The situation was thereafter calmed and the boat was lowered away.

It was during these chaotic moments as these boats were being lowered that the occurrence of a suicide was said to have taken place.

The incident was covered in a May 14, 1912, article in the *London Daily Telegraph* which was taken from a letter written by third class passenger Eugene Daly to his sister in Ireland.

As a boat from the Cabin Deck was being lowered, Daly stated that an officer pointed his gun and declared that if any man tried to get in the boat, he would shoot him on the spot. He then saw the officer shoot two men as they attempted to get into the boat. After that Daly heard another shot and he saw the officer lying on the deck. Daly was told that the officer had shot himself but he only heard the shot and did not see the shooting.

This incident was also believed to have been described by First Class passenger George Rheims in a letter to his wife dated April 19, 1912. The letter was revealed in *The Titanic, the Psychic and the Sea*, by Rustie Brown.

Rheims stated that he saw an officer shoot and kill a man that was attempting to get into the last boat as it was leaving. As there was nothing else for him to do, Rheims said the officer told us, "Gentlemen, each man for himself. Good-bye." After that, Rheims related, he offered a salute and then fired a bullet into his head.

Soon after the event, two accounts of the incident were introduced separately. While they came from two different sources who were not acquainted with each other, they did not identify who the officer was.

Sixth Officer Moody was atop the roof of the officer's quarters working to free Collapsible A, First Officer Murdoch was on the boat deck in charge of lowering the last forward starboard boats, and Chief Officer Wilde was overseeing the loading of Collapsible D on the port side. All three of these officers were lost.

Although these three officers were attending to their duties in the area alluded to by Daly and Rheims, there is no solid proof pointing to which one of them might have shot himself. And yet there is evidence strongly suggesting that there was a suicide.

What must have been one of the most harrowing experiences suffered by the many survivors struggling in the frigid water, had to have been that involving Second Officer Lightoller.

At this time the *Titanic*'s bow had just taken a definite downward plunge creating a surge of water that sloshed up to the forward wall of the bridge. This created a powerful wave that washed people back in a swarming torrent of freezing water.

Lightoller was atop the officer's quarters as the bow was sinking and the stern of the vessel was rising increasingly higher out of the water.

It was as if he felt a thousand knife wounds puncture his skin when he entered the 28° water. His first thought was to try and reach the crow's nest which was normally a hundred feet above the deck, but was now visible just above the rising sea. Nearly in shock he swam toward the crow's nest but then realized that it too was part of the ship and it would sink as well.

Finding it very difficult to swim, he realized that he was weighted down by the heavy Webley revolver that was still in his pocket, so he quickly threw the pistol to the depths. At this time sea water was pouring down the stokeholds through the fiddley gratings located behind the bridge and around the forward funnel. On the boat deck in front of this funnel was a twenty by fifteen-foot, rectangular air vent shaft, with a thin wire grating affixed over the top. The grating served as a screen to prevent trash from being sucked down the vent.

The shaft led directly down to No. 3 stokehold, having a straight drop of nearly 100 feet all the way down to the bottom of the ship.

In his horror, Lightoller was sucked down and held on top of this wire grating with the rush of sea water pouring over him as the ship was sinking. Pinned there fast against the thin grating by the sheer force of the water pouring into this opening, he was terrorized with what would happen to him should the frail grating give way.

Struggling and kicking to get clear, near drowning,

his lungs were at the bursting point.

It was then that a great blast of hot air from deep within the ship shot up the shaft blowing him off the grating and up to the surface of the sea.

Once more engulfed in the whirlpool that surrounded him he was again drawn back to a similar perilous position against the fiddley gratings. Almost out of air and about to give up, he was once again somehow released from the deadly grasp. He was then sent bursting to the surface within reach of the Collapsible that he had earlier launched from atop the officers' quarters.

It was one of the most panic-stricken and frightful tales of any of those who survived.

During the British Inquiry, held in Westminister, England, from May 2nd to July 30, 1912, Mr. W. D. Harbinson represented relatives of some of the third-class passengers who were lost on the *Titanic*. He issued this statement at the end of his testimony:

I wish to say distinctly that no evidence has been given in the course of this case which would substantiate a charge that any attempt was made to keep back the third-class passengers. I desire further to say that there is no evidence that when they did reach the boat deck there was any discrimination practiced either by the officers or the sailors in putting them into the boats.

Thus the matter was closed and was therefore concluded with the closing statement by the Right Honorable Lord Mersey, Wreck Commissioner:

I am satisfied that the explanation of the excessive proportion of third-class passengers lost is not to be found in the suggestion that the third-class passengers were in any way unfairly treated. They were not unfairly treated.

Had third-class passenger Daniel Buckley, a twenty-one year old Irishman, been present at the British inquiry he would have strongly begged to differ.

In Buckley's testimony at the Senate Inquiry, he told a somewhat dramatic and different story.

After discovering that water was coming in the steerage quarters, he heard stewards shouting, "All up on deck unless you want to get drowned."

He and a group of other steerage passengers scurried topside to find another crewman about to lock the gate at the top of the steps that led from the forward well deck up to the first-class deck. Buckley describes what happened:

Senator Smith: Were you permitted to go on up to the top deck without any interference?

Mr. Buckley: Yes sir. They tried to keep us down at first on our steerage deck. They did not want us to go up to the first-class place at all.

Senator Smith: Who tried to do that?

Mr. Buckley: I can not say who they were. I think they were sailors.

Senator Smith: What happened then? Did the steerage passengers try to get out?

Mr. Buckley: Yes; they did. There was one steerage passenger there, and he was getting up the steps, and just as he was going in a little gate a fellow came along and chucked him down; threw him down into the steerage place. This fellow got excited, and he ran after him, and he could not find him. He got up over the little gate. He did not find him.

Senator Smith: What gate do you mean?

Mr. Buckley: A little gate at the top of the stairs going up into the first class deck.

Senator Smith: There was a gate between the steerage and the first-class deck?

Mr. Buckley: Yes. The first-class deck was higher up than the steerage deck, and there were some steps leading up to it; 9 or 10 steps, and a gate just at the top of the steps.

Senator Smith: Was the gate locked?

Mr. Buckley: It was not locked at the time we made the attempt to get up there, but a sailor, or whoever he was, locked it. So that this fellow that went up after him broke the lock on it, and he went after the fellow that threw him down. He said if he could get hold of him he would throw him into the ocean.

Once on the boat deck, the group realized that many lifeboats had already been lowered, and No. 4 lifeboat forward on the port side was about to be sent down.

A number of men got into this boat, but were ordered to get out by an officer.

Buckley was able to remain, because Mrs. Astor, also in that boat, covered him with her shawl, thereby concealing him.

According to the British Inquiry, this boat was lowered at 1:55 a.m. It was second to the last boat lowered.

There were also other instances of locked gates and the prevention of steerage passengers' entry into higher class areas.

Third-class passenger Olaus Abelseth related in his Senate inquiry testimony that he saw many steerage passengers climbing up and along one of the cranes. From there they ventured over the railings to access the boat deck. Otherwise entry into that area was closed to them.

Abelseth was fortunate to find his way through to the first-class area to eventually get aboard an early boat. As there were no women around when it was loaded, he and several men sprang into the boat.

Some steerage passengers made it to the boats; others did not. For the most part, by the time these third-class passengers who were saved made it to the boats, most of the boats were gone. Only a few instances are recorded in relation to steerage passengers being prevented from entering an area for access to the boats. However, only 174 men, women, and children third-class passengers were saved out of the 710 aboard. In reviewing these figures, one wonders if there were not many other incidents where these passengers were denied access to the boats as well.

What is so shockingly ironic is the fact that while so many of these steerage passengers were detained, and experiencing great difficulty getting topside to the boats, many of those very boats left the *Titanic* only half-filled. It was known that there was a language barrier and many wives were not willing to leave their husbands. This may explain why so few of the third-class passengers were saved.

It has been written and asserted that there was no procedure that restricted *Titanic*'s third-class passengers; however, there was no procedure to begin with. Other than the accepted practice of the time, which may have been in place and followed more strictly on other vessels, there were no procedure or guidelines to follow on the *Titanic*.

What procedure should one follow in case of emergency? What route should one take to assemble at what lifeboat? In what order will the lifeboats be filled? On the *Titanic* there was no set order, no procedure, no guidelines, and no lifeboat drill for practice. This was completely contrary to the accepted practice of the time.

By the time the lifeboats were being lowered, the *Titanic* had taken on a port list which meant that the lifeboats on that side of the ship leaned out and away from the side, leaving a wide gap between the lifeboat and the rail of the ship. Lifeboats on the starboard side were leaning into the side of the ship bumping against rivets as they were lowered.

Crossing the gap to the port boats presented a problem, especially for those wary passengers afraid of heights. Those willing to board boats on the starboard side had a frightful time too as it was necessary to push the boats away with oars so that the protruding rivets did not hinder the lowering.

On top of this dilemma, as *Titanic*'s bow sank lower and the stern of the ship rose higher, the boats near the bow were close to the water, but the ones further aft were sent down from a frightening height.

Some idea of the problems, confusion, and lack of procedure associated with the lowering of the boats is related in Second Officer Lightoller's account in the Senate Inquiry pertaining to the lowering of boat No. 4:

We had previously lowered a boat from A Deck, one deck below. That was through my fault. It was the first boat I had lowered. I was intending to put the passengers in from A Deck. On lowering the boat I found that the windows were closed; so I sent someone down to open the windows and carried on with the other boats, but decided it was not worth while lowering them down - that I could manage just as well from the Boat Deck. When I came forward from the other boats I loaded that boat from A Deck by getting the women out through the windows. My idea in filling the boats there was because there was a wire hawser running along the side of the ship for coaling purposes and it was handy to tie the boat in to hold it so that nobody could drop between the side of the boat and the ship.

Some boats were lowered in a haphazard manner with either the bow or the aft end tilting down at such an angle as to practically spill its occupants out. One boat was lowered directly on top of one already in the water. The rope lines used for the lowering of the boats, in some cases had to be cut. There was difficulty because the tackle connecting those lines to the boats could not be unhooked.

All this confusion and difficulty could have been avoided had lifeboat lowering drills, guidelines, and procedures been covered and instilled in the crew during trials.

Only lifeboat No. 14, under the command of Fifth

Officer Lowe, returned to the scene to pick up survivors. From around the wreckage four people were taken aboard, one of which died. By this time, most of those in the water had succumbed to the freezing water and froze to death.

Those fortunate enough to have gotten away from the *Titanic* in lifeboats feared being swamped by those victims still in the water after the vessel sank.

There was also the unfounded fear of being sucked down with the vessel as it sank. Other than the frightful experience that Officer Lightoller had after being sucked down, nothing like that occurred when the vessel went under. It was said that after the *Titanic* sank, there was actually a wave that pushed people away, rather than a suction that could have pulled them down.

Those who could put their fears aside, and wanted, even demanded that their boat return, were either over-ruled by the majority who did not want to return or by the crew member in command of the boat.

There were those too who claimed they did not return because they were bent on rowing toward the lights of a ship in the distance. Their intention was to reach that vessel and return with it to render aid.

As cold-hearted as it seemed, out of the mass of bodies afloat, Lowe's efforts concentrated on those still determined to be alive.

In an article in *The Semi-Monthly Magazine*, May 1912, Third-class passenger, Mrs. Charlotte Collyer who was in No. 14 lifeboat related a remarkable story.

She told of a Japanese man who was discovered lying face down on a floating door. He had secured himself in place with rope. He was thought to be dead. The sea was washing over him and those in the boat could see that he was as stiff as the board he was on.

They called out to the man and received no response, so there seemed nothing to do but search for those possibly still alive.

"What's the use?" said Officer Lowe.

"He's dead, likely, and if he isn't there's others better worth saving than a Jap!"

The boat was pulled away, but for some reason Officer Lowe returned to this Japanese man and hauled him aboard. One of the ladies in the boat began rubbing his chest, while some of the others rubbed his hands and feet.

Astoundingly, after just a few moments of this aid, the little man opened his eyes and spoke in his native tongue. It appeared as though he was wanting to convey that yes, indeed he was alive. He managed to stand up, and with his arms above his head, moved about in the confined space, and stamped his feet. He had almost completely recovered his strength in only a few moments.

One of the sailors nearby, who was so exhausted from pulling on his oar, was pushed aside by the recovered man. The little Oriental man took his oar and rowed in earnest until the boat was picked up.

Officer Lowe who watched all of this with his mouth agape was heard to say, "By Jove! I'm ashamed of what I said about the little blighter. I'd save the likes o' him six times over if I got the chance."

Who knows what you will do in that kind of situation. Will you take the chance to save your fellow-man, or take the easy way to save your own skin?

If you returned in your lifeboat that night, to pick up survivors while they were alive, almost for certain you stood the chance of being swamped. Some accounts tell us of those heartless few who kept others from entering their boats; and even struck those in the water with oars to keep them away.

Looking back, we might say that yes, we would have returned to pick up those helpless ones. But how can we know the trauma and fear that was witnessed that night. In those awful moments, it might have been better to ask the Almighty what to do. You would then know what to do according to what you heard in your heart from His guidance. Either that, or be haunted by the screams of those you did not help.

Chapter Eleven
The Last True Story

Few would know the reason why,
The seasoned captain had to try.
In desperation way back then,
He started Titanic up again.

It happened. As surely as there was a *Titanic,* it happened. What follows is perhaps the most incredible saga you will ever read about the great ship. It is the story of how and why the *Titanic* was started up again—an ill-fated manoeuvre—after hitting the iceberg. Hidden in the testimony of surviving crew members during the Senate inquiry, and from passenger accounts and statements in era newspapers, this disastrous start-up was scarcely mentioned and never elaborated upon.

To those up close who scrutinized and analyzed the tragedy at the time, the incident was preposterous. However, it did happen, and it is even more preposterous to the post-event experts and scholars, who know more fully the breadth of *Titanic*'s hull damage and the aftermath of this seemingly absurd decision.

I will take you back aboard the *Titanic* that night and walk you through the events surrounding this critical time as reported by a surviving second-class passenger Lawrence Beesley, a young science teacher at Dulwich College in London, who was aboard the *Titanic* en route to America for a vacation.

Beesley's account, The Loss of the S. S. *Titanic*: Its Story and Its Lessons, considered one of the most credible studies of the disaster, was published in 1912. His account serves as the nucleus of this drama, and the primary absolute proof that the start-up happened. It is combined with corroborating events and statements from other passengers and crew members, and is presented in a chronological sequence to prove the feasibility of the episode.

The story will offer proof that this incredible manoeuvre actually took place. This evidence will also reveal that had the *Titanic* not moved on again, quite possibly everyone aboard could have been saved. At the very least many more of those who perished could have been rescued.

Because I am a marine artist who has studied maritime history for most of my life, you can imagine how thrilled I was on April 15, 1983, to be selected as part of the crew of the Jack Grimm *Titanic* Search. Like countless other *Titanic* enthusiasts, I had devoured everything available about the vessel, which was unquestionably the most renowned maritime legend of all time.

As project artist and historian, my job would be to capture the *Titanic* in multiple panoramic views as she lay on the ocean floor. The artwork was to be based upon the mission's film footage and still photography.

In January of that year, I was first informed by Mr. Grimm that he would consider my joining the group. Even though I was not yet accepted, I began working on my contribution to the project. At that time no one had a clue as to how or in what position the *Titanic* was lying. But I knew that we could expect very limited visibility at the *Titanic*'s depth. I also knew that no matter how sophisticated the underwater cameras were, they could not possibly reveal the entire mass of the enormous vessel in panoramic view. But with the photographic data acquired from the mission, I could accomplish those panoramic views—piecing them together with my artwork—and Mr. Grimm was interested.

So, to get a head start on my work, I started making preparatory drawings of the *Titanic* from every possible view imaginable. I nearly went crazy in the process. Finally, I found help through a design company, with a Cadds 4 computer program, that worked with me to develop 464 different drawings of the *Titanic* from virtually every possible angle that she might be resting in. It was like viewing the *Titanic* from all these positions on the ocean floor, on paper. These drawings were deemed highly crucial for on-site study, and they became my ticket to joining in the search.

However, a more intense and broadened study of the *Titanic*, brought about because of my participation in the expedition, led me to this fascinating story which no else seemed to have, as of yet, discovered.

I remember one day on the search when the whole crew was sitting together in the conference room aboard the research vessel *Robert Conrad* contemplating what our next move would be. We had not yet found the *Titanic*. Frustration was running high, gales continued to hamper the mission, we had lost valuable equipment, and we were about to give up the search. In the end, I took the information I had gathered regarding this incredible story and formulated my own theory. Guessing that the wreck was not where it was supposed to be because of the start-up incident I had learned of purely by chance, I asked if anyone had ever heard the story of how the *Titanic* had been started up again after striking the iceberg.

There was dead silence for a moment as everyone stared at me in disbelief at the question. I felt awkward, realizing that none of them knew of the incident. I could also see by the way they looked at me that they thought the idea was ridiculous. But inside I knew I was right.

Lawrence Beesley had written it all down with precise details. Indeed, his account was praised as the most thorough non-technical chronicle of the structural defects of the *Titanic* which had ever been produced. One can gather from his writing his keen attention to fact and desire for precision.

The details in Beesley's book are as follows. After dinner on the night of the disaster, April 14, 1912, we find Mr. Beesley in the saloon with a hundred or so other passengers singing hymns. Leading the group was a young Scotsman who sought suggestions from the others as to which to sing. Among the many favorites chosen, it seemed strange to Beesley at the time that many of the selections were associated with the dangers of sea travel. He later would poignantly remember the reverent and impassioned tone of the crowd as they sang, "For Those in Peril on The Sea."

Beesley retired to his cabin at about 10:45 p.m. He was pleased to have secured a double-berthed cabin, D-56, three decks below the top, or boat deck, near the saloon, and nicely situated for access to other parts of the ship.

As he sat on his sofa undressing, his bare feet on the floor, he noted how he could feel the distinct vibration from the engines through the metal almost directly below his cabin. He compared this with the same vibration he felt in his bath when he placed his hands on the side of the tub. He climbed into his top berth and settled down to read from 11:15 p.m. until the *Titanic* struck the iceberg at 11:40 p.m.

By 11:15, most of the passengers had already settled down for the night, and the only audible sounds were the pleasant hum of the engines, and stewards attending to their tasks up and down the corridors.

Beesley continued reading until he felt what he thought was merely an extra heave of the engines and a slightly more than usual jiggle of the mattress on which he sat. There was no sound to indicate a crash, no jar, and no sense of fear. Soon after, he experienced the same thing again, but thought it had been brought on by an increase in the speed of the engines.

Meanwhile, down below in Boiler Room No. 6, there was anything but calm as a fireman, Frederick Barrett, saw an explosion of green seawater burst through the side of the hull about "two feet above the floor plates, shearing the starboard wall the entire length of Number 6 and slightly into the coal bunker in Number 5." Time: 11:40 p.m., April 14, 1912.

Regretfully, recent exploration of the bow section where the damage occurred did not and cannot reveal the true configuration of the *Titanic*'s wounds, because the damaged lower portion of her hull is buried in the ocean bottom. But the best calculation of the size and length of the gash, rupture, tear, hole, wound, or whatever you choose to call it comes from Edward Wilding, a respected naval architect, and head draftsman at Harland and Wolff at the time the *Titanic* was built. Needless to say, the *Titanic* had been his pet project.

His estimate, based on eye-witness reports, revealed the length of the damage to be two-hundred and forty-nine feet from Hold No. 1 all the way back to an area two feet into Boiler Room No. 5. The iceberg, he noted, had penetrated more than three feet into Hold No. 1, causing an enormous hole in the ship.

In testimony given in the British Inquiry on June 6, 1912, Edward Wilding related in detail the extent of the hull damage near Hold No. 1.:

Mr. S. A. T. Rowlatt (counsel on behalf of the British Board of Trade): You know there has been evidence that water was flowing into the fireman's passage at the bottom of the spiral staircase?

Wilding: There was.

Mr. Rowlatt: Was the fireman's passage at any such point in contact with the outside skin of the ship?

Wilding: No, it was 3 feet 6 inches - I have a plan showing it.

Lord Mersey (Wreck Commissioner): 3 feet 6 inches what - away from the ship? I should have thought it was much further than that.

Wilding: I have a plan showing it (produces plan).

Lord Mersey: Now I understand it.

Mr. Rowlatt: Would you look at this blue print for a moment, Mr. Wilding? You show here the two spiral staircases?

Wilding: Yes, two spiral staircases, one port and one starboard.

Mr. Rowlatt: Now, on either side of those [staircases] there is an upright white line representing a division, is there not?

Wilding: A watertight wall.

Mr. Rowlatt: Is that a watertight wall?

Wilding: Yes, it is a watertight wall to the trunk containing the stair, the side wall.

Mr. Rowlatt: And the 3 feet 6 inches that you mention is that from the corner at the bottom of that watertight wall to the skin of the ship?

Wilding: I think it scales a little less, about 3 feet 3 inches from the corner horizontally to the shell of the ship.

Mr. Rowlatt: Is that the nearest point at which that cavity in which the spiral staircases are approaches to the skin of the ship?

Wilding: That is right.

Mr. Rowlatt: So that is it a fair deduction to say that if water from the sea was running into that spiral staircase space something must have penetrated the ship through the skin for 3 feet 3 inches, and then through iron, the thickness of which you will tell us by and bye, of the watertight compartment again? - That it must have come far enough in through the side of the ship to disturb effectively that watertight wall?

Lord Mersey: In other words, the ice must have penetrated into the ship more at this point than 3 feet 6 inches.

Mr. Rowlatt: Yes, and have penetrated in sufficient bulk to break this partition at the end of the 3 feet. It must have been a good heavy sharp piece that succeeded in coming in as far as this in order to do further damage. (To Edward Wilding) Is not that so?

Wilding: It probably came in gradually. It started some few feet further forward and came in gradually; I do not think it went in with a bang.

Mr. Rowlatt: You do not think the puncture was necessarily confined to this spot in the vessel?

Lord Mersey: No, no; but at that spot there must have been a puncture which penetrated at least 3 feet 6 inches into the ship at that point.

Mr. Rowlatt: How much further forward than that we cannot say?

Wilding: No, we cannot say, but we know damage was done in the 4 feet. My Lord, we put a mark upon the model, if you remember, at the time down here, as showing the position, when [Leading Fireman] Hendrickson's evidence was given. I remember that.

Lord Mersey: And that, you say, is where the ice penetrated if there was water in the tunnel as described. It was there that the ice would have penetrated and have admitted the water?

Wilding: That is right.

It is from this testimony that we know that the iceberg penetrated *Titanic*'s hull at least three and a half feet at Hold No. 1, close to the forepeak. While it is impossible to determine the exact configuration of that wound, it was certainly a gaping puncture large enough to have admitted a spur of the iceberg deep enough into the hull to damage the wall alongside the starboard winding staircase.

Contemporary theory would suggest that the iceberg had probably punctured, bumped, and scraped along the vessel to create the wounds to the *side* of the *Titanic*. It is interesting to note, and important to point out, that nearly every account of the disaster will tell you that the damage was sustained to the *side* of the *Titanic*. But in fact, it definitely occurred near the forepeak on the bow as well. (see drawing in pictorial section). Because of the curvature of the vessel, the side of the hull was also that area immediately at the bow. This neglected fact—an enormous hole at the bow—made steaming on again a critical and horrendous mistake, as I shall demonstrate later in this chapter.

Without noticing anything unusual, Beesley continued reading for a few more moments until he felt the engines slow and finally stop. This is another critical point to bear in mind, for critics of this start-up theory have said that the *Titanic* did not stop after hitting the iceberg, but rather coasted to a stop before sinking. However, shortly after striking the iceberg, *Titanic*'s engines were reversed bringing her to a complete stop.

The vibration through the metal, and slight bouncing motion on Beesley's mattress which he had felt for days suddenly ceased. Thinking that the ship might have lost a propeller blade, he slipped on his robe and shoes and went into the corridor, where he asked a steward why they had stopped.

The steward did not know but voiced no concern over the matter. Beesley, intrigued with every aspect of his exciting vacation, climbed three flights of stairs to the top deck and talked with another passenger. He then descended to the deck below, conversed with several others in a smoking room, and returned to his cabin to read again.

After a short while he heard people walking in the corridor and decided to go up on deck once more. This time, because of the biting cold, he donned a heavy jacket and trousers. For several minutes, he noticed more passengers walking about and seeking information.

Searching for a cause of the delay, he looked over the rail and down at the sea to discover that "the ship had now resumed her course, moving very slowly through the water with a little white line of foam on each side. I think we were all glad to see this: it seemed better than standing still."

It is apparent from this statement ("the ship *had now* resumed her course"—my emphasis) that the *Titanic* was already under way again when he looked over the side, although it is impossible to determine exactly when she had started again or how long she had been moving again when Beesley had looked over the side.

Allowing for his movements and conversation, the time would have been about 12:15 a.m., April 15th.

Second Officer Charles Lightoller, the senior-ranking surviving officer of the disaster, when later answering questions posed by Senator Fletcher in the Senate inquiry, offered the following information regarding the start-up:

Senator Fletcher: What did the boat do first? Did she tremble, did she shake, did she keep on her course, or what was the immediate effect? Was she obstructed?

Mr. Lightoller: I do not know. I was in my berth. I do not know what course she kept on. There was a slight shock.

Senator Fletcher: You were awake?

Mr. Lightoller: Yes.

Senator Fletcher: What was the immediate effect?

Mr. Lightoller: A slight shock, a slight trembling, and a grinding sound. She did not make any alteration to her course, so far as I am aware.

Senator Fletcher: So far as you could see, the blow did not come from beneath the surface, but came straight along the ship?

Mr. Lightoller: I could not see anything. . . .

Senator Fletcher: But so far as you could feel?

Mr. Lightoller: So far as I could feel, there was a slight shock and a grinding sound. That was all there was to it. There was no listing, no plunging, diving, or anything else.

Senator Fletcher: What was done then with reference to the ship? Was her speed lessened then?

Mr. Lightoller: I was below; I do not know anything about that.

Senator Fletcher: You could not tell that?

Mr. Lightoller: I could not tell you officially. I know I came out on deck and noticed that her speed was lessened, yes.

Senator Fletcher: Was she not actually stopped entirely from going forward?

Mr. Lightoller: No, she was not. That is why I said, in my previous testimony, that the ship was apparently going slowly, and I saw the first officer and the captain on the bridge, and I judged that there was nothing further to do.

Also questioned during the Senate inquiry, by Senator Burton, Quartermaster Alfred Oliver, who was on the bridge when the collision occurred, testified that the *Titanic* had been ordered ahead at half speed (approximately 12.37 MPH).

Senator Burton: Were the engines reversed? Was she backed?

Mr. Oliver: Not whilst I was on the bridge. But whilst on the bridge we went ahead, after she struck; she went half speed ahead.

Senator Burton: Who gave the order?

Mr. Oliver: The captain telegraphed half speed ahead.

From there on Senator Burton, for some unknown reason, all but dropped that line of questioning. How I would have loved to have been there at that time to ask the proper and important questions and press for answers to those questions. It is most unfortunate that this inquiry was conducted by those who apparently had little knowledge of or experience with the sea and the marine field. Furthermore Bruce Ismay, the officers, and crewmen, most likely afraid that their answers would be incriminatory, were not that free with their responses.

When concerned survivor Edwina (Troutt) McKenzie asked the *Titanic*'s purser what was wrong with the ship (chapter 5), he told her, "We've just stopped for a while, but we're moving on again."

Further evidence of the start-up comes from *Titanic* Survivor Miss Caroline Bonnell, who wrote an article that appeared in the *Columbus* (Ohio) *Citizen*, on April 19, 1912.

Miss Bonnell related that upon returning from an upper deck, accompanied by her cousin, Natalie Wick, they were told by an officer to "go below and put on your lifebelts—you may need them later."

On the way to their cabin, the two girls told Miss Bonnell's aunt and uncle, Mr. and Mrs. George Wick, what they had been told to do.

Mr. Wick just laughed at them and said, "What, that's nonsense girls, this boat is all right. She's going along finely. She just got a glancing blow, I guess."

We must carefully consider the time involved in Beesley's next movements, about 12:15 a.m. Although noticing, without any undue alarm, a lifeboat being uncovered, Beesley decided to go below again. Upon doing so, he noticed an ever-so-slight downward tilt at the bow, which he ascertained no one else had noticed. He further related in his book that the only way he could confirm this downward tilt was when he descended the stairs. A sense of being unable to put his foot down in the right place on the step made him feel as though something was out of balance.

He descended to D deck, where his cabin was located, and came upon two ladies concerned about why the *Titanic* had stopped.

"Oh! Why have we stopped?" they asked.

"We did stop, but we are now going on again," Beesley answered.

"Oh, no," one of the ladies replied, "I cannot feel the

engines as I usually do, or hear them. Listen!"

Beesley remembered how he had noted earlier that the vibration from the engines was most noticeable in the bathtub, where the throb came through the metal from the engines below. So he ushered the ladies down the corridor, located a vacant room, and took them into a bathroom and had them place their hands on the side of the tub. Upon doing so, they were much relieved to feel the engines working below, and realized they were making some headway.

Beesley left the ladies and went to his cabin, where he passed some stewards in the saloon. He carefully noted their lack of alarm and calm attitude. Near his cabin he came upon and conversed with a man who was fastening his tie.

"Anything fresh?" he asked.

"Not much," Beesley answered. "We are going ahead slowly and she is down a little at the bows, but I don't think it is anything serious."

"Come in and look at this man," the man laughed. "He won't get up."

Beesley looked in on the man in the top berth who had his back to them and was wrapped in his blankets with only his head visible.

"Why won't he get up? Is he asleep?" Beesley asked.

The man in bed grunted and said, "You don't catch me leaving a warm bed to go up on that cold deck at midnight. I know better than that."

They both jokingly told the man that he had better get up, but he was satisfied in believing everything was safe, and that all the fuss was quite unnecessary.

Returning to his cabin, Beesley put on some undergarments and sat on his sofa to read for some ten minutes, when he heard the loud command from above: "All passengers on deck with life belts on."

He gathered his reading material, picked up his life belt and jacket, and went to the top deck once more. On the way, he met other passengers, none of whom appeared alarmed.

One lady, however, amused him by frightenedly squeezing his arm when she asked him for help in finding her life belt. Kindly locating a steward who found her a life belt, he eventually reached the boat deck to find many passengers assembled there.

Feeling once again the ice-chilled air, Beesley noticed that "even the breeze caused by the ship's motion had died entirely away, for the engines had stopped again and the *Titanic* lay peacefully on the surface of the sea." The time was now about 12:45 a.m.

The time spent by Beesley in his stateroom, ascending and descending stairs, talking with and assisting other passengers *after* he noticed the *Titanic* had started up again (about 12:15 a.m.), until he was on deck the third time to realize the vessel had again stopped (about 12:45 a.m.), was about thirty minutes. It appears quite logical, then, that the *Titanic* had steamed on for at least twenty minutes during this interval of at least thirty minutes.

Therefore, for twenty minutes or more, massive amounts of seawater were driven forcefully into that enormous hole in her bow, thus gravely reducing, second by second, minute by minute, the precious time she had left before sinking.

Edward Wilding, the naval architect at Harland and Wolff, calculated that sixteen thousand cubic feet of water entered the *Titanic* in the first forty minutes after striking the iceberg. One has to believe that he based this calculation on the *Titanic* remaining static, not moving forward, for few believed that she had moved on.

Using Wilding's calculations, and converting that sixteen thousand cubic feet of water into figures that we can more closely associate with, it would have meant that in forty minutes almost five hundred tons of water, at the rate of 12.48

tons per minute entered the ship. That would have been nearly three thousand gallons a minute, or over 1,040 pounds every second! These converted figures are also based on the weight of fresh rather than salt water which, would have been even heavier.

Taking these figures into account, one can more clearly imagine the horrific volume of sea that entered her wounds while the *Titanic* was under-way.

The relatively short time the supposedly unsinkable *Titanic* remained on top of the water after hitting the iceberg has always intrigued me. The time seemed so dreadfully short when I compared it with the time frame of another famous sea disaster: the *Andrea Doria-Stockholm* collision. In this regard a startling comparison can be seen that dramatically points to the danger of making headway with a holed vessel.

This tragedy occurred at 11:10 p.m. on July 25, 1956, off Nantucket Island. Interestingly, because of her alleged water-tight integrity, the *Andrea Doria* also acquired the fabled distinction of being unsinkable.

First, let us keep in mind that the *Titanic* remained on top of the water for only two hours and forty minutes after striking the iceberg.

The Swedish-American liner *Stockholm* struck the starboard broadside of the Italian Line *Andrea Doria* and drove her icebreaker-reinforced bow thirty feet into the *Andrea Doria*'s side, creating a v-shaped gash fifty feet wide at her upper deck that narrowed to a point deep below the water level. Within minutes, the *Andrea Doria*'s A deck was beneath the water, and she listed so heavily to starboard that her port lifeboats became immediately useless. Although the *Andrea Doria* sustained a vertical wound to her side rather than a horizontal wound like the *Titanic*'s, one could surmise that because the *Andrea Doria* took on this immediate and severe list, she was holed far worse than the *Titanic*. Yet she remained on top of the water until 10:09 a.m. the following morning—only one minute shy of eleven hours!

Why? I believe it was because she did not attempt— could not attempt—to move on again.

Critics have also come forward to declare that the *Andrea Doria* was a smaller vessel with different watertight integrity, that the configuration of her wound was different, etc., etc. All moot points. The one fact to keep in mind is that regardless of all the other relevant or irrelevant givens, the *Andrea Doria* had to have had a more serious wound because of her immediate and severe list.

What on earth had Captain Smith been doing? Why would he further endanger the lives of those aboard by resorting to this absurd manoeuvre? Had he been attempting to steam toward the lights of a ship seen off the port bow and later estimated by Second Officer Lightoller to have only been a couple of miles away?

Under command of Captain Stanley Lord, the four-hundred and forty-six foot Leyland Line steamer *Californian* had departed Liverpool April 5th bound for Boston. At 10:30 p.m. that night, this vessel had stopped for the night, surrounded by a large field of loose ice.

Captain Lord had related to his third officer his observance of a light from an approaching vessel east of his position. His wireless operator had then offered that the only vessel in their vicinity was the *Titanic*. By 11:30 p.m. Lord could see the green starboard sidelight of the vessel and estimated her to be about five miles away, still to the east of him.

Officer Lightoller related in his account that a number of passengers had approached him, asking if the situation aboard was serious. He tried to calm them by saying that it was only a matter of precaution to get the lifeboats ready and in the water in case of an emergency. At any rate, he had further advised them that they were perfectly safe because there was a ship only a few miles away, and then pointed to the lights of that ship off the port bow. They could see the lights as well as he could.

Lord had ordered his third officer Groves to contact the ship by Morse lamp, which Groves had done, but without receiving any response.

When the *Californian*'s Second Officer Herbert Stone came on watch after midnight, he too attempted to signal the vessel by Morse lamp, but again received no response. Apprentice James Gibson, also on the bridge, received no response from his efforts to signal. By this time Captain Lord had retired to his nearby chart room to rest.

Beginning around 12:45 a.m., Stone observed bright white lights in the sky which he first thought to be shooting stars. As many as eight white rockets were observed by the *Californian*'s officers, with no action taken to render aid. Gibson reportedly roused Captain Lord with word of all the rockets, and was asked if he was certain of their color. However, in a sworn statement, Captain Lord stated that he was not visited by Gibson at that time. Since the rockets were white instead of red, it was thought that they were perhaps in celebration of the vessel's maiden voyage.

And so, as the *Titanic* was sinking, and in need of immediate assistance, the *Californian*'s wireless operator was asleep with his receiver turned off.

Captain Lord was chastised for the rest of his life for not responding to those desperate distress signals.

During this most critical time Captain Smith was trying to get his vessel to safety.

Can you imagine the shock and disbelief on the Senate floor when that seemingly ridiculous answer—"The Captain telegraphed half speed ahead."—was given by Quartermaster Oliver? Even today, those unfamiliar with maritime common knowledge, practice, and procedure ask the same question.

Captain Smith, seasoned veteran that he was, had been doing exactly what he had been trained to do in a crisis. He had been attempting to get his wounded vessel in shallow water, or at least closer to another ship for assistance, quite possibly the *Californian*, seen earlier off the bow. It is what any experienced mariner would do today under similar circumstances. Smith knew he was some three hundred and fifty miles from the nearest landfall, Cape Race, Newfoundland. But in desperation he had decided to make the attempt.

Just as he knew how many fingers he had, he was also well aware of how critically few lifeboats he had at his disposal, and the appalling consequences that would likely follow. Most agonizing of all perhaps, would have been the haunting thoughts of iceberg warnings he so blatantly disregarded earlier.

Lastly, under his command, he was facing the possibility of losing the grandest vessel in existence, along with the assured blemish that would stain his character should his vessel founder.

Most certainly during his career he had known of other vessels which had been in serious situations and close to foundering that were miraculously saved. Therefore, there would have been no question in his mind but that he had to try to reach shallow water and possibly beach his ship, or at least attempt that manoeuvre.

As these thoughts undoubtedly raced through his mind, he staved off the high potential of total panic, remained calm and level-headed, and pursued the only alternative his sea experience would have directed him to do. He moved his vessel forward with the slim hope she could maintain headway long enough to reach safety.

In the interim, the ship was examined and soon pronounced able to remain afloat, but for only a frightfully short while longer. He then stopped for the final time and began procedures for the lowering of lifeboats. There is no record of any change in course. There was never an order given to abandon ship, a decision highly criticized, but one which surely prevented outright panic.

Second Officer Lightoller, in his account, *Titanic*, writes about beaching the *Titanic* had it remained afloat. Lightoller relates how the *Titanic*'s fate was doomed when the fifth compartment, counting from forward, was smashed in by the iceberg.

He stated that, "Even with three or four of her forward compartments full of water, the margin of safety would have made it fairly certain that she would still have floated: The whole ship would have assumed a fairly acute and mighty uncomfortable angle, yet, even so, she would, in all probability have floated—at least for some considerable time, perhaps all day. Certainly for sufficient time for everyone to be rescued; and, just possibly until she could have been beached."

When Third Officer Herbert Pitman was asked in the Senate inquiry about cries in the water after the *Titanic* sank, he stated "There was a continual moan for about an hour."

Edwina (Troutt) McKenzie (chapter 5) stated that you could hear voices or screams in the water for an hour or more after the *Titanic* sank.

Adding that hour to the sinking time of 2:20 a.m. gives you 3:20 a.m. It is outright staggering to realize that the rescue ship *Carpathia* arrived on the scene at 4:05 a.m.—only forty-five minutes later!

Forty-five minutes. It seems such a narrow span of time, unless, of course, you happened to have been in an open lifeboat in that chilled air or afloat in the freezing water.

Had the *Titanic* not steamed on again after the collision, even if she had done so for just a few moments, the *Carpathia* might have reached the scene in time to save many more lives—perhaps in time to have rescued everyone from the sinking vessel, perhaps even in time to witness the sinking of the great liner after all were safely aboard.

Survival is a strange thing. To survive, one must have the hope and the will to survive. During one of my many lectures on this story, a very skeptical doctor in the audience challenged me as to how those people could have possibly stayed alive in that freezing water for forty-five minutes.

I could offer no reasonable explanation except to tell him it was due to the tenacious and steadfast will to survive. I then gave him two miraculous examples.

The Great Lakes are widely known for their fierce and famed November storms. In November 1958, the bulk-carrier *Carl D. Bradley* sank in northern Lake Michigan with the loss of thirty-three lives. There were four survivors. Two were lost during that horrible night, but two others survived for fourteen hours on an open raft, in freezing temperatures, wearing only light clothing. Frank Mays, now the sole survivor of that tragedy, prayed for fourteen hours non-stop, and was rescued with ice in his hair and his clothes frozen as hard as a brick.

"Miracle man" Dennis Hale survived another Great Lakes disaster when the *Daniel J. Morrell* sank in Lake Huron on November 29, 1966, with the loss of twenty-nine lives. Covered with icicles, Hale was rescued from his open raft after thirty-eight hours wearing nothing more than a pea coat and undershorts.

Quite possibly none of *Titanic*'s passengers would have even had to have been in those frigid waters if the *Carpathia* had arrived on the scene early enough. Lifeboats from both vessels could then have been utilized to shuttle passengers to safety.

How many more *Titanic* passengers would have been saved if they had been given the hope and the will to survive by seeing the *Carpathia* there on the scene earlier? How many more of those countless victims clinging to wreckage or floating with life belts in the freezing water would have been saved if the life of the sinking *Titanic* could have been extended for just a little while longer? How many more would have been saved had the *Titanic* not steamed on again?

Epilogue

It can easily be said that the *Titanic* disaster resulted in the greatest loss of life directly attributed to the greatest comedy of errors.

When those Irish laborers secretly sealed that lucky coin in her keel bidding her good luck, they must have known she would need all the extra favors fate could offer, knowing she would not be christened. When the launch was further blemished by a death associated with the event, those who built her knew she was marked with the indelible stain of an unlucky ship.

Today, most of those old launching practices are forgotten, but even those who are just a little superstitious, are wont to proclaim, "No wonder she sank," when they discover that the great ship had a marred launch.

It was said that no cost was spared to build her, yet pennies were pinched when it came to providing adequate measures for lifesaving. Bulkhead design flaws that allowed sea water to flow freely from compartment to compartment as the vessel sank at the bow guaranteed her demise. Bloated with over-confidence, her owners rushed her into service without the shipboard gear and guidelines that could have prevented the tragedy. The proper number of lifeboats, a search-light, binoculars, lifeboat drills, and emergency procedures would have made the difference.

As her rich and famous passengers basked in their luxury and the lower classes were confined to their spaces, she dashed for a speed record while her captain foolishly ignored iceberg warnings.

The fateful collision hardly jarred the ship, but it surely jarred the world, and in the few hours that followed the true character of the heroes, cowards, and victims she carried was laid bare.

After the great ship was holed by the iceberg, it came to a stop, but in a last ditch attempt to facilitate a rescue, Captain Smith ran on again at half-speed. Not knowing the extent of damage, experience guided him in a desperate effort to reach landfall, or at least to get closer to the *Californian*, visible only a few miles distant. Although Captain Smith was in the right with this manoeuvre, it was a fatal error that accelerated the sinking and gravely shortened *Titanic*'s life, thereby negating any chance of the *Carpathia* to reach her before foundering.

Out of the one-thousand five hundred and seventeen casualties, even the one-hundred and fifty seven women and children who were lost did not make it to the lifeboats, some of which left barely full. Because of the fear of being swamped or sucked down with the sinking ship, only a single boat returned to aid those in the freezing water.

The screams for help not only haunted those who did not offer aid, but served to forever remind mankind of its callous and shameful arrogance.

The End

Maritime History in Art

LAT 42° 50.4' N, LO 82° 28.8' W

http://www.jclary.com

Meet the author

The prolific and unquestionable talent of marine artist, author, and historian Jim Clary is traced to his early days as a schoolboy. He remembers vividly having his ears boxed for drawing in arithmetic class. However, his love for the sea and ships no doubt began during his early years when he lived near the Detroit River, fishing and playing amid the sea gulls and the beckoning whistles of passing vessels. This environment he believes, established his strong desire to study and paint maritime history.

When the family moved to the rural town of Richmond, Michigan, Jim spent much of his time in nearby St. Clair, a small town along the St. Clair River, which deepened his interest in ship's lore and led him to devote his full talents to painting ships and collecting bits and pieces of maritime history.

Like most of the famous marine artists of the past, Clary is self-taught. Hungry for and fascinated by maritime lore, his natural talent evolved through the combined practice of drawing and the love and knowledge of ships. Thus having relied on extensive study and experience, his works are profound statements of historical accuracy and articulate detail - a trademark that made him famous.

During his endless hunt for research material in old news articles, libraries, museums, or private photograph collections, he usually finds new and startling facts or long forgotten details. His "cracker barrel" interviews with old-timers have uncovered many fascinating anecdotes and his conversations with survivors of the *Titanic* or other disasters have often provided him with inside information unattainable through normal sources.

Much of his knowledge comes from personal experience. Passage on Great Lakes ore carriers and ocean-going vessels have provided him with the opportunity to witness, first hand, the saga of the sailing ship era, today's modern behemoths, the chill of a ferocious high seas gales, and Great Lakes November storms. His staging of a battle on the USS *Constitution* in which U.S. Navy men assisted him in reenacting a deck fighting scene gave him invaluable reference for his painting of the only pictorial record of what it looked like on *Old Ironsides* during the heat of battle. His hook landing on and visit to the deployed aircraft carrier USS *Enterprise* CVN-65, enabled him to better capture realism in his painting of the World War II, USS *Enterprise* CV-6 in a kamikaze attack.

Having a great regard for the connoisseur of maritime history, the same dedication to detail and accuracy which has earned Jim Clary renown among marine museums and collectors throughout the United States and abroad, enabled him to be chosen as expedition historian and artist for the 1983 *Titanic* search.

Because many of his "finds" were just too fascinating to put away again in some dusty file, he shares his knowledge through his writing. His best selling books, *Ladies of the Lakes I* and *II, Superstitions of the Sea*, and his latest volume, *The Last True Story of Titanic* have proven to be just as compelling as his art.

Jim Clary has realized his boyhood dream of bringing "ghost" ships to life through art. He is a man who made himself, who thrives on art, and who thrives on the notion that others will enjoy and learn from his work for years to come.

Maritime History in Art - 201 N. Riverside - St. Clair, MI 48079 - 810-329-7744
http://www.jclary.com

Great Historical Fiction from Domhan Books:

All prices effective Autumn 1998 and are in Us dollars and pounds sterling

A Most Secret Device by David Shaw $12.95/6.99
An alternative history - what if the transistor had been invented in England in 1936 instead of in America in 1946? Would the British Empire still be an historical relic, or would it be where Bill Gates would be now if he'd left Harvard already owning one quarter of the planet and one sixth of its population?

An Experience in Four Movements by Lidmila Sovakova $10.00/£4.99
This is a historical puzzle situated in the seventeenth century. Its pieces reconstruct the infatuation of a Poet with a Princess, culminating in the death of the Poet, and the retreat of the Princess within the walls of a monastery.

The Sea of Love by Sorcha Mac Murrough hardcover $25.00/£14.00 paperback $15.00/£8.00
Ireland 1546
Wrongfully accused of murder, Aidanna O'Flaherty's only ally against her evil brother-in-law Donal is the dashing English-bred aristocrat Declan Burke. Saving him from certain death, they fall in love, only to be separated when Declan is falsely accused of treason. Languishing in the Tower, Declan is powerless to assist his beloved Aidanna as she undertakes an epic struggle to expose her enemy and save her family and friends. She must race against time to prevent all she loves from being swept aside in a thunderous tide of foreign invasion....

The Wizard Woman by Shanna Murchison hardcover $25.00/£14.00 paperback $15.00/£8.00
Ireland 1169
The great Celtic myth of the Wheel of Fate is played out against the backdrop of the first Norman invasion of Ireland in 1169. Dairinn is made the wizard's woman, chosen by the gods to be the wife of the handsome but mysterious Senan. Through him she discovers her own innate powers, and the truth behind her family history. She must bargain with the Morrigan, the goddess of death, if she is ever to achieve happiness with the man she loves. But how high a price will she have to pay for Senan's life?

Hunger for Love by Sorcha MacMurrough $12.95/£6.99
Ireland and Canada, 1847
Emer Nugent and her family are evicted from their home at the height
of the Potato Famine in Ireland. Forced to emigrate to Canada, they
endure a harrowing journey on board a coffin ship bound for Grosse
Ile. Emer, working as a cabin boy to help her family's financial
situation, meets the enigmatic Dalton Randolph, the ship's only
gentleman passenger, who is not all that he seems. They fall in love,
but darker forces are at work against them. Emer's duty to her family
forces Dalton and she to separate. Will they ever be able to overcome
the obstacles in their path to true love?
This incredible saga of love, adventure and intrigue continues in the
second volume The Hungry Heart, also available from Domhan Books.

The Hungry Heart by Sorcha MacMurrough $12.95/£6.99
Canada and Ireland 1847-1849
Emer Nugent leaves her lover Dalton Randall to search for her family
in the hell of the Grosse Ile quarantine station. The land of opportunity
is nearly the death of them all. Dalton is deceived into thinking Emer is
dead by his father, and is about to marry the daughter of a business
rival when he meets Emer again. Outraged that his plans for keeping
the two apart have failed, Dalton's father has Emer arrested on false
charges and transported back to Ireland.
But the Ireland she returns to is on the brink of civil war. Emer finds
herself unwittingly embroiled in the 1848 rebellion, and is put on trial
for her life. Dalton must travel half way across the world to try to save
her before it is too late.
This incredible saga of love and adventure begins with the first volume,
Hunger for Love, also available from Domhan Books

Scars Upon Her Heart by Sorcha MacMurrough $12.95/£6.99
Lady Vevina Joyce and her brother Wilfred are forced to flee Ireland
after being falsely accused of treason. On the road with Wellington's
army, they meet an unexpected ally in the enigmatic Major Stewart
Fitzgerald. Side by side they fight with their comrades in some of the
most bitter battles of the Napoleonic Wars. Can Vevina clear her name,
protect those she loves, and stop the Grand Army from taking over the
whole of Europe in a bold and daring move engineered by the person
responsible for her family's disgrace?
Is Stewart really all that he seems? Appearances can be deceptive....

If you enjoy historical works of fiction and non-fiction, why not also look for these books from Domhan?

USA: Domhan Books, 9511 Shore Road, Suite 514, Brooklyn, NY 11209

Internationally: Domhan Books, 3 Killyvilly Grove, Enniskillen, Co. Fermanagh BT 74 4RT, N. Ireland

Natchez by Deb Crockett $12.95/ £6.99
The Hungry Heart by Sorcha Mac Murrough $12.95/ £6.99
Scars Upon Her Heart by Sorcha Mac Murrough $12.95/ £6.99
The Sea of Love by Sorcha Mac Murrough-hardcover $25.00/ £14.00
The Wizard Woman by Shanna Murchison-hardcover $25.00/ £14.00
A Most Secret Device by David Shaw $12.95/ £6.99
An Experience in Four Movements by Lidmila Sovakova $10.00/ £4.99

Please add $4.95/£3.00 for postage and handling. Please allow 28 days for delivery.
Please note that all prices are in US dollars and pounds sterling. Please debit myACCESS, VISA, MASTERCARD, AMEX a total of

Expiry Date _ _ _ _ _ _   Signature _ _ _ _ _ _ _ _ _ _ _ _ _ _ _ _ _
Name:

Address:

☐ **Please add me to your mailing list.**